Yiddish Genesis

Essays

Richard J. Fein

YIDDISH GENESIS

Editor: Clarinda Harriss
Graphic design: Ace Kieffer
Front cover art: Marc Chagall
Author photo: Stanley Sagov

BrickHouse Books, Inc. 2012
306 Suffolk Road
Baltimore, MD 21218

Distributor: Itasca Books, Inc.

ISBN: 978-1-938144-04-2

Printed in the United States of America

Books by Richard J. Fein

Poetry

Selected Poems of Yankev Glatshteyn (translations)

Kafka's Ear

At the Turkish Bath

To Move into the House

Ice like Morsels

I Think of Our Lives: New and Selected Poems

Mother Tongue

Reversion

With Everything We've Got (translations)

B'KLYN

Prose

Robert Lowell

The Dance of Leah

Acknowledgment is made to the editors of the following journals in which the following essays have appeared, sometimes in slightly different form:

Congress Monthly: "Jew, Poet"

Jewish Currents: "Waiting for Yiddish"

Midstream: "The Jewish Story," "The Beginning-End of Yiddish"

Orim: "The Companion-Translator"

Reconstructionist: "The Jewish Story Revisited"

Shofar: "What Can Yiddish Mean to an American Poet?"

Yiddish: "The Navel of the Bialy: Yiddish Poetry and the Needs of a Translator"

The etching on the cover, by Marc Chagall, "The Creation of Man," from his Bibical etchings, is used with the permission of the Haggerty Museum of Art, Marquette University.

Note: I want to thank Teresa Iverson, whose sensitive reading was vital to the making of this book (to the point of my having stolen from her an occasional phrase).

For Sholem Beinfeld and Shimen Kass

"Not a book of articles, a book of genesis . . . "

Marina Tsvetayeva, *Letters: Summer 1926*

Preface

This book could not have been written without obsessions that go back to my childhood and that then re-emerge as findings of the adult I became. When obsessions have obtained a voice, they then can shape experience. Whatever the conceptions and chimeras that rove here, I ride them to travel more deeply into Yiddish and Genesis. I have entered and re-entered my materials as ways of enabling me to claim them, or them to claim me—not so different from the way my poetry works.

I have also come to see that a goodly part of the book deals, directly or indirectly, with translation. The chemistries of translation and reflection on that process have entered my life and my engagement with poetry. It is not sidework for me, but part of whatever development I might claim. Translation is for me a form of second birth.

These essays are visitations of Jewish literatures long haunting me. I am also a reader trying to understand himself—explication as double events, extending over decades. To adapt a Chagallian image, I eye the horse that eyes me in my village of memory and reading.

Table of Contents

I

The Jewish Story

> "I was so happy to learn that you were Russian!
> I consider myself a Russian, you understand. As a Jew, I am also
> a German, a Frenchman, a Pole, I am all Europe—but a Russian
> foremost."

In the story "The Hand that Fed Me," by Isaac Rosenfeld, these words were written by one Joseph Feigenbaum, also known as J. F., or Joe, or Feigenbaum, or Joseph in a letter he sends to a girl named Ellen, who may or may not exist, and who, even if she does, may or may not remember him, as she hasn't seen him in years.

I will not get closer to understanding the Jewish short story than what I have just said. But I will, like a narrator of a Sholom Aleichem monologue, continue to talk.

Let me retell an anecdote (actually an old Jewish joke with variant settings) from Meyer Liben's title story in *Justice Hunger:*

> So when the man came back, after thirty years of reflection on
> life's meaning with the conclusion that "life is like a fountain"
> and was questioned as to *why* life was like a fountain, he
> immediately replied, *"So it's not like a fountain."*

A man makes a tour of the world only to end up where he began. He goes nowhere and makes a tour of the world. This is a ghetto wisdom. It bites itself. In that anecdote about a man's absolute reliance on and then absolute distrust of mental constructions, you have the hidden springs of the Jewish story.

Defining the Jewish story is out of the question. So let me tell you how you recognize one. A Jewish story has a horse in it. That old Jewish joke about the elephant and the Jewish problem had it wrong. It's the horse.

Reflect on these matters:

Tervye, Sholom Aleichem's dairyman, often talks to his horse. The horse listens. Who else really listens to him? Who else understands him? The reader, maybe. If so, and there is no horse in the Jewish story, the reader is the horse.

In Sholem Asch's story "The Sinner," the sinner, who is also an inside-out holy man, has a way with horses. They keep the Sabbath together and take walks in the meadow. "And this walk of theirs," we are told, "is more acceptable to God, blessed is He, than repeating 'Bless the Lord, O my soul!'"

In Isaac Babel's story entitled, naturally, "The Story of a Horse," the narrator expresses grief over a fellow Cossack who is leaving the service, apparently because he has six wounds, but actually because he has had his darling horse, the white stallion he trained and fed, unfairly taken away from him by a superior officer. The narrator, presumably someone like Babel, says at the end that he missed his friend: "We were both shaken by the same passions. Both of us looked on the world as a meadow in May—a meadow traversed by women and horses." (Often in his war tales, Babel deepens the pathos by placing his half-hidden Jewish narrator into a Homeric-Cossack ethos.)

In his introduction to Babel's *Collected Stories,* Lionel Trilling has a shrewd and sympathetic discussion of Babel's life and art, his urge to join the Cossacks and participate in (or look upon) the boldness, the grace, the indifference, and the horror of their violence. It's as if Babel wanted to learn to master the beast that rode over him and his people.

On his way to Kiev, Yakov Bok, in Bernard Malamud's *The Fixer,* takes out his rage on his stubborn, non-conforming, even non-horse horse: "I'm a bitter man, you bastard horse. Come to your senses or you'll suffer." Malamud makes one feel that the horse in turn would speak to Bok, warning *him.*

What kind of intimacy is this between horse and man in a Jewish story? Horses have burdens. Horses can be beautiful, reared only for the sport of life. Horses can also be terribly old, plodding along in blindness and reins. Why do homes for old people remind us of homes for old horses? And why do Jewish writers have the conviction that horses are such good listeners?

The problem doubles back on itself. In the parable, "A Horse," by Isaac Rosenfeld (who came closest to being an American Kafka, Leslie Fiedler once observed), we are told that a soldier who owned a horse "talked and the horse listened and understood, which makes a conversation." But then, to put the shoe on the other foot, the horse falls in love with a girl, who first pets him but then slams the door in his face when he comes around to court her. The horse has only himself to talk to; the soldier-owner doesn't understand the plight of his horse, who moans:

> All my life I was admired as a horse; but now that I am in love, I am treated as a monster. Is there something monstrous in being in love? That cannot be. Then is there something monstrous in being a horse? Now that I am in love, it must be so. But how can I help being in love, since I am free to love? Is it my fault I am free? Am I to blame that I'm a horse? But how can I remain content with being a horse? Oh this burden, heavier than any I ever carried on my back!

The horse finds it difficult to enlist the sympathies of his uncaring owner who has his own row to hoe as far as women are concerned. Though adept at self-exegesis, the horse cannot fully understand himself. He breaks his leg and expects the soldier to shoot him now.

One begins to understand why there are horses so often in Chagall's paintings of Vitebsk or some imagined village. We see horses who merge with a man's eye, who lie down with maidens, horses whose manes are made of our dreams. A beautiful woman can be a horse. A man can fly through the air like a horse. A village can be the horse of our imagination. On the back of a horse a man rides into life.

Cossacks also rode into villages on horses. Chagall, like Babel, seeks to master them.

It is not hard to see why so many Yiddish writers found in

Chekhov a man to model their work on, a man to learn from. For Chekhov wrote the supreme horse story, "Misery," subtitled, of course, "To Whom Shall I Tell My Grief?" a story often copied. Iona Potapov, the sledge-driver, cannot find anyone among his customers willing to listen to his woes—his son has died. At the end of the story, at night, Iona goes out to the barn and shares his sorrow with his horse: "The little mare munches, listens, and breathes on her master's hands. Iona is carried away and tells her all about it." Chekhov is one of the great Jewish writers.

In Saul Bellow's novella, *Seize the Day,* Tommy Wilhelm needs a horse to talk to. But there aren't any on the streets of the Upper West Side. So he cries his heart out to a dead man in a funeral parlor. The mute understand. Horses understand. Yet all of man's speech is to himself. Is there anyone else who listens? Combine the horse from the Jewish short story and Bellow's dead man and you have God's mute mercy, His infinite, ignorant listening which moves the talking man to tears.

II

For years I have been trying to figure out what makes a Jewish story Jewish, and not only that, but why Chekhov is one of the great "Jewish" writers, and furthermore, why Russian literature is so close to Jewish literature. I have been trying to find a critical way of expressing the nature of the Jewish story, and then one day I re-read an essay about Sherwood Anderson that I had read decades before when I was an undergraduate. The essay was written by Robert Morss Lovett. He says that like Chekhov, Anderson

allows no pattern or structure to interfere with the immediate appeal of fact. Western art of fiction or of the stage tends to be centripetal; it draws attention to a group of characters whose interrelations develop into a plot. In Russian stories and plays,

22

such as *The Cherry Orchard*, the action is centrifugal; it diffuses attention and carries it beyond the immediate action to more remote implications of life that is unrevealed but none the less significant.

Lovett notes that many of Anderson's stories deal with frustration in human life that arises from isolation, from the difficulty or inability of one person to enter into an understanding with another. Classic Russian literature, like Gogol's "The Overcoat," Dostoevsky's "Notes from the Underground," and Tolstoy's "The Death of Ivan Ilych" are written out of some implacable sense of loneliness and suggest the centrifugal rather than the centripetal pattern of fiction. Jewish stories are too—the ones with horses.

In place of those "interrelations [that] develop the plot," Anderson, like Chekhov, gives us a sense of diffuse, more remote implications of life.* If we take this idea and see it in terms of the Jew's traditional relationship to social and government authority in Europe, we see why the Jew's loneliness, a loneliness on the scale of a people in exile, impelled many of its finest writers to write in terms of what Lovett calls the centrifugal art of fiction. Lacking political power, undergoing some eternal loneliness and ever-present hostility, and knowing that his people exist and suffer in their present place by the whims of history, the Jewish writer searches for the story's final setting just over the edge of that order the rest of the world takes for granted and thrives on, an order that threatens the Jew.

Sholom Aleichem is the master of this condition. The absurd situations in his world are sometimes a mockery of the

---

* Anderson, by the way, figured that the reason he was often considered as being under the Russian influence was that he, like characters in Russian literature and like Russian writers themselves, was raised largely on cabbage soup. In the forward to *Studies in Classic American Literature,* D. H. Lawrence separates Anderson from American writers: "And by American I do not mean Sherwood Anderson, who is so Russian."

supposed order the normal, outside world inhabits. Yet the Jewish outlandishness is also our own kind of identity, our homegrown privilege. In the forward to *Inside Kasrilevke*, translated by Isidore Goldstick (New York, 1965), Sholom Aleichem announces:

> Of recent years all sorts of books about cities and lands and similar useful subjects have made their appearance in other languages. So I've said to myself, We imitate other peoples in everything: they print newspapers—so do we; they have Christmas trees—so do we; they celebrate New Year's—so do we—Now, they publish guidebooks to their important cities . . . why shouldn't we get out "A Guide to Kasrilevke"?

And such a guide! It's a guide to disorder that mocks *their* order, but above all, it is a disorder that is ours, that *we* created and was not visited upon us by their order. If Kasrilevke can survive itself, it can survive anything. (If Chelm can survive its "wise" men, it can survive the machinations of any government leaders. If a Jew can survive a Jewish waiter, he can survive whatever the world serves up to him.) And Providence must be looking over Kasrilevke and Jewish towns like it, despite their misfortunes—how else could the places survive their absurd situations, their tenuous hold on order? Indeed, Sholom Aleichem's stories, like some of those towns, survive in spite of themselves—that is the secret of their art. His stories seem to be stories in exile from what a story ought to be, as if they don't know how to behave like a story. That very kind of exile is the clue to their special survival. Jewish stories have their forms and attitudes for very good reasons.

Russian and Jewish literature (of the late 19th and early 20th centuries) seem to have so much in common that one often gets the feeling that Russian literature was written by a bunch of renegade Jews. Dostoevsky's stories like Sholom Aleichem's seem on the verge of bursting apart.

One of the attractions of Russian literature, maybe its greatest attraction, lies in its moral concern and moral directness that *seemingly* destroy any pretense of aesthetic distance or construction. One reads a Russian story as one bites into a roll—it's impossible to keep the crumbs off yourself. Russian stories seem to say, "I'm all over you; there's no distance between us." Reading Sholom Aleichem is like eating.

The Russian story and the Jewish story unite in their aesthetic of crumbs, in their refusal to sweep up everything into some final aesthetic, in their reluctance to make a final structure out of a horde of unruly facts, in their feeling that out of any of those facts, or crumbs, a man may make a speech of moving self-mockery and transfiguration.

In reading Russian and Jewish stories one gets the feeling, to change the metaphor, that stories are threadbare overcoats so that everything whirling around the outside can come through. The aesthetic of the Russian and Jewish story is in that overcoat that shelters and lets everything through. The stories and their themes are by nature concerned with exposure, and survival is conceived as being possible only within the terms of that exposure. Russian literature is attractive to Jews because it, like Jewish literature, informs us that our vulnerabilities are what make us human.

Kafka is the supreme Jewish writer. You think of the centrifugal art and then remember that Kafka's two great novels as well as many of his tales are unfinished (or feel that way) and create channels "Beyond the immediate action to more remote implications of life that is unrevealed but none the less significant."

Kafka's stories are archetypes of the Jewish story. His tales are blessed runes of the pure Jewish story, in form as well as content. His brief parable "Before the Law," in which a man spends his entire manhood before a doorkeeper who blocks his way to the Law and whom he cannot get past, is the epitome of the Jewish story, the religious cousin of such classic Jewish tales as I. L. Peretz's "Bontsha the Silent" and Isaac Bashevis Singer's "Gimpel the Fool." In such a basic Jewish story, the character's life has trained him (mournfully in the case of Bontsha, but with a sacred foolishness in the case of Gimpel) to make spiritual capital out of his personal and social powerlessness. But even as the author exploits his character's weaknesses with great pathos, he tells us in the story—don't think that life in the process hasn't taken its revenge on this character. Kafka's story is also the supreme parable of the Chosen People: Because this door to the Law was meant *only* for you, you will suffer and still not enter. "Before the Law" is a brief tale, its very form like the life of the man it is about, somehow unresolved.

If you can't have the here and now, if you cannot *plot* your existence socially and politically, you can describe a disorder that is your very special arrangement of reality. Or you can pretend that there really is a supra-plot, from above, in which you are history's suffering, unknown, but chosen star. And you can put a man on the roof, or in some other absurd place, above it all, playing a violin in the sky. Or you can place your principal character in exile, and his power to think about his situation is his peculiar brilliance. You pretend you can figure out what life is really like, not by acting in it—"they" restrict you from fully doing that—but by thinking about it; and because you know that what you know is not only your skill but also a substitute for that self-determination you really want, you announce, "Life is like a fountain." And to show how free and bold you are in spirit, you further speculate, "So, life is not like a fountain." Through your mind, and the metaphor it makes and destroys, you have summed up life by understanding it. You have surpassed it, and have made a joke of your abilities to do so. Meanwhile, life remains what it has been, doing to you what it has been doing all along.

III

The theory of the short story is short and imperfect, though art is long and examples of it are many.

In his informal and idiosyncratic study of the short story, *The Lonely Voice,* Frank O'Connor looks upon Gogol's "The Overcoat" as the key work in understanding the short story. He sees Turgenev's famous phrase about Russian writers, "We all came out from under Gogol's 'Overcoat,'" as also being a general truth about stories. He quotes a long passage from the story, a passage in which the chief character, the poor downtrodden clerk, Akaky Akakievich, bewails his fate. A new clerk in the office joins in the game of baiting Akakievich, but then feels guilty and imagines the clerk before him, uttering, "Leave me alone! Why do you insult me? . . . I am your brother." The new clerk, through the words he imagines he hears from another character there before him, learns to feel for this other man. (Melville in his tale "Bartleby," as we can see, has at once written a great Russian and a great Jewish story and is history's unrecognized midwife to Kafka.) O'Connor says that if he wanted another title for his study of the short story, he would have chosen the words "I am your brother." Some titles of books of short stories by Jewish writers in America: *Justice Hunger, Idiot's First, The Little Disturbances of Man, A Pile of Stones, Nickel Miseries.* They all come out from under the "Overcoat."

Does the Jewish story as I have explored it here include biblical writings, stories like Jonah and Tobit? Yes. The stories of David and of the prophets and of military victories and of heroes like Samson? No, probably not. Yet the story of Hosea fits. The story of a man who in order to serve God married a whore could have been written by Bernard Malamud. In fact it was, only he re-wrote it a bit and called it "The Magic Barrel." Above all, I have been talking about the Jewish story of Eastern Europe, no matter where it is written.

1968

The Jewish Story Revisited

What are you building?—I want to dig a subterranean passage.
—Franz Kafka, *Parables and Paradoxes*

About six years ago I wrote an article called "The Jewish Story," in which I argued that one could recognize a Jewish story because it had a horse in it. The article, to steal John Updike's brilliant pun description of his novel *Bech*, was a *jeu d'esprit*. It turned out that I could refer to a number of Jewish stories with horses in them to document my theory. Since then my theory has been verified by my discovery of even more works than I was aware of at the time I wrote the article, like Mendele's *The Nag* and Sholom Aleichem's "Methuselah, A Jewish Horse." The latest confirmation of my theory appears in the form of Bernard Malamud's story "Talking Horse." Malamud's fable dramatizes the idea attributed to the great Hassid, the Maggid of Mezeritch, who once informed a visitor, "The horse who knows he is a horse, is not. Man's major task is to learn that he is not a horse."

An unexpected graphic analogue of my argument appeared in a drawing by David Levine in the *New York Review of Books.* For illustration of some posthumous material by Isaac Babel, Levine drew Babel wearing a Cossack hat, with his perennial granny glasses, sitting on a horse. The horse was hoof-pecking at a typewriter. Then to my surprise I found scholarly support for my theory in an article entitled "The Horse Dealers' Language of the Swiss Jews in Endingen and Lengau," by Florence Guggenheim-Grünberg, to be found in a book titled (conveniently for my theory) *The Field of Yiddish.*

Further familiarity with the Jewish story, however, convinces me that I must extend my theory. Since my intention is to be a guide to the question, "How do you know a Jewish story when you see one?" I now must conclude that if a story doesn't have a horse in it you shouldn't jump to the conclusion that it is not a Jewish story. It still may be one if it contains one other element, and that is a seemingly endless and guarded passageway leading inevitably to some authority that is rarely reached.

The quintessential stories representing this Jewish type are Kafka's "Before the Law" (a part of *The Trial* but also printed separately) and "An Imperial Message." "Before the Law" is a famous description of a man who spends his whole life unable to get past a doorkeeper who stands before an endless succession of doors and still other doorkeepers leading to the Law. Needless to say, since we are dealing with a Kafka story, the poor man never does get past all those doors and doorkeepers to reach the Law. The story can be read as Kafka's own inability to reach the Torah. The important people at the synagogue, standing on the *bimah,* prevent him from opening the door and reaching the Law. They can't assist him and he doesn't know how to reach the Law by himself.

"Before the Law" can also be seen as Kafka's brief, bitter capitulation of the Jews, who were assigned a special entrance to the Law and could not get through to it. At the end of the tale, the doorkeeper yells at the dying man: "No one else could be admitted here, since this gate was made only for you. I am now going to shut it." The story is also Jewish in that it evokes the traditional Diaspora situation, the Jewish separation from ultimate political and secular authority. I also realize that "Before the Law" can be interpreted as a comment on Protestant loneliness (each man has his own way to God). The point at which the Jewish predicament blends with the modern predicament is part of the seamless web of meaning in Kafka's stories. For Jews Kafka has double revelations. Kafka's *The Castle,* I believe, reminded Franz Rosenzweig of the Hebrew Bible.

The other Kafka story that contains the passageway theme is "An Imperial Message." It is the story of the Emperor's messenger who carries to "you" a message from the dying Emperor (God?). But the messenger can't make his way out of the palace in order to deliver his message. The message will never be received. If the man in "Before the Law" can't get inside the door, the messenger in this tale can't get out the door. The way to the Law is blocked; the way back from the Law is blocked. Such might be abstract religious readings of these tales. On another level, as I said before, these tales are about the inability of the Jews of the Diaspora to connect with a supreme secular authority. Buber observes that "Kafka's contribution to the metaphysics of the 'door' is known. . . ."

It is curious how a Kafka tale can be considered a dark version of a tale by the Wise Men of Chelm. In particular, "Before the Law" and "An Imperial Message" resemble the Chelm story "When the Czar's Son Becomes Sick." In this story, not about the typical idiotic ratiocination of Chelm's wise leaders but about the "nature" of political arrangements, a doctor cannot get through the palace bureaucracy to reach the bedroom of the Czar's son before he dies. The Czar ends up suffering from his own system. This tale projects onto the Czar and his family the helplessness before arbitrary authorities that Jews themselves experienced constantly in Eastern Europe. In a book of Chelm stories,* this tale is illustrated by a picture of an imperiously dressed guard with a hand raised, preventing a doctor (who could also be a Jewish merchant or scholar) from going through. The picture brings to mind Kafka's "Before the Law."

Both of Kafka's stories, by the way, prefigure one of the favorite skits of Jack Benny's radio program. After the miserly Benny makes the difficult decision of going into his vault to take out some money, the word resounds down vast hallways that Mr. Benny is coming down to the cave-like vault. Guard after guard echoes down the deep passageway the cry of Benny's desire and impending appearance. Thus many radio listeners became familiar with Benny's version of the same motif used by Kafka; only in the case of Benny, the way was made open and money replaced the Law.

Sholom Aleichem also contributed an episode to the Jewish-passageway motif. The *luftmensch* Menakhem-Mendel is thinking of buying some mines. But how to pull off such a big deal? Whom can

---

* *The Wise Men of Chelm,* edited by Samuel Tenenbaum, New York: Thomas Yoseloff, 1965.

he approach to make an offer to go in with him on this operation? Menakhem-Mendel wonders:

> To whom can one offer such a big deal? Brodsky, naturally! So there is another snag: How does one break into Brodsky's office? First of all, in front of the door stands a doorman with bright buttons who looks you all over to see how you're dressed—a shabby coat is given no entrance. And then if, God willing, you do manage to bypass the doorman, you have to wait about six hours on the staircase before the Lord takes pity on you and you are granted a glimpse of Brodsky passing by. And if you have the good luck to lay your eyes on him, the chances are that he whizzes past you like an arrow, and before you have time to turn around, he is already sitting in his carriage and—hail and farewell! So you have to be polite enough to return the next day. The next day the show starts all over again—and no wonder, considering how many affairs he has to deal with! So it isn't very easy to get to him, but I haven't lost hope someday to break through, and then we can get down to business.

I quote from *The Adventures of Menahem-Mendl*, translated by Tamara Kahana (New York, 1969), so you will get the flavor of this theme as treated by Sholom Aleichem, but also feel its kinship with Kafka's grimmer version of the same theme. There is one universe where the Kafka seeker, the doctor to the Czar's palace, the Menakhem-Mendel of the above passage and Sholom Aleichem's Teyve are wandering, or standing, with degrees of forlornness and hope, before impenetrable doorways.

Let me give you one contemporary example, because you should not think that the passageway theme is no longer in use. One recent version is Bernard Malamud's title story "Idiots First."

In this version the dying Mendel must get his idiot son, Isaac, onto a train to California so that Isaac can be taken care of by Mendel's uncle, who is himself eighty-one years old. But Mendel first must get money for the train fare. He goes to the pawnbroker and pawns a watch, but doesn't get enough money for the ticket. Then

31

he goes to Fishbein the philanthropist, whom he finally gets to see, that is, after getting his way past Levinson, the servant-doorkeeper. Fishbein offers a meal to Mendel and Isaac but sticks to his policy: "I never give to unorganized charity." The father and son leave for the home of the rabbi, who has no money but who gives up a coat for the worthy purpose. Mendel and Isaac flee for the pawnbroker's with the coat while the complaining wife screams at them for taking advantage of her husband's charity. They arrive at the train station just before the train is to depart. Mendel is forced to argue with "the uniformed ticket collector" (you recognize him this time?) to let them through even though the gate is closed. Mendel engages him, as we say, in a dialogue and tries to get him to pity them.

It turns out that this ticket taker is a figure named Ginzberg who haunts the story and is himself pursuing Mendel. In fact, Mendel must get Isaac on that train before Ginzberg does something to Mendel that Mendel cannot finally escape. Mendel argues with Ginzberg, the ticket taker-gate keeper, who only relents after he gets a glimpse of his angry, negative self in Mendel's eyes. For the second time in the story the guard at the door relents, and Isaac is allowed to get on the train going to California. Malamud's story is a striking version of the passageway theme because in it Ginzberg, seeing how pitiless and awful he can be, relents. Like Abraham, Moses, Jonah and Job, Mendel argues with Ginzberg-God-Grim Reaper. In Malamud's version the traveler makes it through the passageway, though Ginzberg the gatekeeper may lurk around the next bend, behind the next door.

To sum up, these closed doors, labyrinths and inaccessible passageways are all representing the Diaspora condition of the Jews in relation to both God and secular authority. God himself sometimes seems to block the way. These images of an uncompleted journey also suggest the idea of the Jews as a people looking for their home, or seeking a renewal of some divine authorization.

Since the above-mentioned stories have prompted me to amend my earlier theory, I affirm my new one: A story does not have to have a horse in it in order to be Jewish. It is also a Jewish story if it has a passageway that it is impossible, or at least difficult, to traverse in order to reach the intended goal or authority. The ultimate Jewish story, it would seem, is about a horse in a labyrinth. To the best of my knowledge it has not yet been written.

1974

II

The Companion-Translator

The urge to translate presses after the recognition of affinities in the foreign poem; then that urge turns into a process of brooding and sifting, brooding and sifting in order to shape the qualities of one's own language that will match the effects and inclinations of the poem in the foreign language. There is no inspired translation without the translator having been struck by the original, without his being called to translate it. The translator finds in the original an extension of himself, a dimension of himself conveyed in the other language that must be brought home. The translator finds in the original poem his ego calling back to the surprised discoverer of himself. That is why the translation process is one of simultaneously reaching outward and going inward. In his essay "The Added Artificer," Renato Poggioli shrewdly poses that "like the original poet, the translator is a Narcissus who in this case chooses to contemplate his own likeness not in the spring of nature but in the pool of art."

Translation marriages are made in a compulsive heaven but consummated on earth. The poem in the foreign language prompts the translator to try on for size the words of his own language. The urge to translate (that other level of creation) feeds on the particulars, that recalcitrant, provoking language of the original, on the rich details after the initial spur—"here too I discover myself." The original poem remains itself, while the translation draws its own life from it and from the genius of the translator's own language. Translation is the art of skinning the cat and bringing home the pelt embodying a new "mee-ow."

The translator is no mere conduit of the poem in a foreign tongue. The translator must neither efface himself nor lord it over the original poem—be neither gifted transcriber nor brilliant distorter. Since the translator's sense of his own integrity "is based on both modesty and self-respect," Poggioli affirms, "the ethos of the translator is a perfect blend of humility and pride." "Productive" would perhaps be a keener adjective than "perfect" here, but Poggioli's phrase conveys the tension and balance of the translator.

The task of the translator is neither to imitate (*pace* Dryden and Lowell) nor merely to convey. The art of imitation is really the writing of one's own poems, taking off from the original. Imitation is to poetry what "variations on a theme by" is to music. This art, as with the "reckless" and "free" Robert Lowell (his own adjectives for his venturous imitations), is really the art of creating a new poem that flourishes best when the reader doesn't really know the original, or maybe better yet, knows it badly.

The task of translators is to capture in their language what the poem possesses in the original, what Walter Benjamin means by the echo of the original emerging from the language forest. That echo has its own quiver.

While translators must be thoroughly at home in their own language, they need not necessarily be masters of the original language of the poem. That is why the plaints, whines and score-card accumulations of howlers by Kornei Chukovsky in *The Art of Translation* end up sounding tiresome and beside the point. That is why academics almost always are not inspired translators but must be relied upon by translators for information, cultural orientation, and for corrections of missed meaning, often half-sensed, half misunderstood. The academic specialist is crucial in assisting translators by supplying knowledge. Or to put the matter differently, the academic side of the translator—if he is that chimera, a poet-scholar—writes the explanatory notes as succinctly and accurately as possible, explaining and detailing the historical and cultural background, the key references, all necessary for the reader to comprehend the poem. But that academic part of the self is put aside, or kept in tow, or shrewdly siphoned from, when the translator takes over. To re-work a distinction of Henry James between historian and novelist: the compiler of the notes can't know enough; the translator may know too many words, too much of unnegotiable history. The felicitous scholarly phrasing in the notes may turn into the sophisticated mark of damnation in the poetry itself. The poet who is his own academic knows how both rich and risky is the mingling of his levels of aptitude—as scholar, as translator.

There were times while translating the poetry of Yankev Glatshteyn that I felt I had been raised in English so that I could pursue Yiddish and in that pursuit entice Glatshteyn into my language. It was my fate (*bashert*—I deliberately trot out that stock Yiddish term) to struggle to possess Yiddish so that I could transport Glatshteyn into English, not satisfied until I had released his poetry into the bloodstream of the one language I knew well, the only language I would ever know well. I couldn't, after a certain point, separate my pursuit of Yiddish and my pursuit of Glatshteyn. He conveyed in Yiddish all the turmoil and pleasures of modernism that I myself was swimming in. I would never get over the discovery that it was possible to marshal such complexities in that language which had harassed me in childhood. It came to woo me in middle age with an intellectual allure which my ignorant and vexed younger years had never imagined. I owed Yiddish something. If I did nothing else in English, found nothing else in Yiddish, my contact with Glatshteyn was enough to justify my possession of the one language, my pursuit of the other. Before I ever guessed it, he was the appointed reason I came to learn Yiddish. My former ignorance of Yiddish—still felt too many times—perhaps could only redeem itself by my bringing Glatshteyn to English.

The uncanny juxtaposition of impotence and mastery comes when one is in the heart of the struggle of learning a new language and of translating from one language to another. Those contradictory terms of "impotence" and "mastery," borrowed from Walter Benjamin, were confirmed for me as I enjoyed a Glatshteyn poem, and struggled with it, and rifled through Weinrich's and Harkavy's Yiddish-English dictionaries, prodded and poked until one stubborn-prolific language yielded itself to the other. The impotence-mastery duality (Benjamin's version of what Poggioli means by the translator's modesty and self-respect) would present itself when Dr. Mordkhe Shekhter, linguist and grammarian of Yiddish, would answer my S.O.S. telephone calls and abundantly instruct me in what a Glatshteyn word or phrase means and then in all innocence would conclude, "But of course it's up to you to put that into English." There was mastery, there was impotence, in the heart of knowing the poem. The next task, mine alone, was to coax, bribe, or badger the poem into its alter-ego. O, the quest for similitudes!

In Glatshteyn I found a ghost in real clothing. He invaded my dreams, as if insisting that he take on a shape, or a presence in my imagination. And as with Hamlet, I had been assigned a task by this ghost. I could not duplicate his presence, do exactly what he had done, do exactly what he would do if he were alive (he would have continued to write poems in Yiddish). Could I evince his presence in the poems I wrote? Could I invoke his presence? Could I point to it— there in the English, in the words I used to embody his work and my discovery of it? Could my English—perhaps even our English, since it was provoked and agitated by his Yiddish—convey the reader into his world of poetry? It is not that I wanted to suggest the Yiddish behind the English translation (all I can think of in that regard is a crude English dialect, the sleazy bag of "Yinglish" effects). Rather, the task was to write an English fostered by the original Yiddish. The task was to write a poem in English that would stand on its own but that—I knew to my regret and inspiration—would never have existed without the Yiddish poem having been written in the first place. The task was to write a poem in English that would be the counterpart of the discovery I made in the original. In this process, the translation is the child that leaves the womb yet forever reveals the traces of what shaped it there.

There is a poem by Glatshteyn that conveys in an indirect way the condition of translating poetry. The poem is *"Dray"* (*"Three"*), from Glatshteyn's second book of poems *Fraye ferzn* (*Free Verse*, 1926) and is dedicated to friend and fellow-poet B. Alkvit, who was also known as Alkvit-Blum.

Three*

(for B. Alkvit)

Three straggling on the road stare at the sunset.
A pair of them—and the calf.
With a cigarette butt between his teeth, one of them says,
like an astonished child,
"The sky."
Draws smoke, spits, and is mum.
The second gazes with soft eyes
and something weeps inside him.
Drained of tears, he looks, spits and is mum.
The calf looks up and moans.
Three step quietly on their own shadows
and stare at the sunset.
And in all three words fall asleep,
and around that place where words sleep,
three suns sink in melancholy.
In the pair of them—and the calf.

A touch of internal rhyme (in the original), as well as the repetition, intimate the camaraderie of the experience, as Glatshteyn and Alkvit are tramping along a road or walking across a field in the Catskills. (I insist on the poem taking place there for solid historical reasons, given the vacation habits of immigrant Jews in New York City, but also because the Catskills are not far from where I now live—in other words, where I translate. And there in the Catskills I myself spent many a childhood summer shunning that Yiddish of which I now see Glatshteyn is a master. Yiddish for me is an adult's return and discovery.)

I slip into the role of the companion in the poem and share the scene with friend Glatshteyn, personifying Poggioli's thesis that the translator "is a character who, in finding an author without,

---

* All translations of Yiddish poetry are my own.

finds also the author within, himself." We don't speak to each other, but we share the walk. When he does speak and utters *"Der himl!"*— "The sky"—it is more to himself than to me, but I catch and share his amazement, his being unexpectedly stirred. He swallows his smoke, as if internalizing the dusk. The friend-translator also spits and is mum. What cries in him is akin to the wonder and speech of his friend. The dual response of *"shpayt un shvaygt"* ("spits and is mum") intimates the conception of the poem and its subsequent translation. The first poet in the poem awaits his companions' parallel response. His companions are his counterparts. The moan of the calf, itself echoing the soft crying of the second poet, intones the problem of re-expression—as if the dear groan of Yiddish itself conveys the perplexity of translation; as if the calf, looking at the same scene and at them, moans in sympathy with the problem the translator-companion faces: How to capture that compelling sense of sky to which the first poet has given voice? That calf is also expressive of the physical stirrings of the poem.

The three witnesses "step quietly on their own shadows," as if their joy of discovery is entwined with an inevitable sadness—the joy inseparable from the passing of the joy and the need to seek words to encompass this response within response. The condition of transience is the ache of inspiration. The moment in the poem has become the emblematic moment of the passing of experience. The sleep the words fall into is not the sleep of oblivion or forgetfulness, but a descent into the sacred melancholy of the poem, the sense of fugitive life. The words descend to a depth beyond their regular use, then muster a return.

The three of them are held by the glow of the setting sun. In that splendid fall they register their astonishment, their gulping for words. The imagination is sometimes charged by the irrevocable waning of a period of history, of a personal experience, of a language. It is a curious variation of the Joshua motif—sustenance in the very words which keep the sun in the process of forever setting.

In the pair of them with the calf (the calf being in this poem what a horse's head is to many a Chagall landscape or village scene) there stirs the human longing that language both register their awe of the setting sun and nestle up to a part of the very nature they admire. The words of the poet and his companion-translator must match the moan of the calf. The poet speaks and spits between his teeth (solid channel of poetic diction); the translator has yet to speak. Meanwhile he also looks and spits, priming the pump of the imagination.

Probably there was a calf in the original experience of Glatshteyn and Alkvit—the poem retains tokens of actual experience shimmering in it. Glatshteyn thus keeps in touch with the original scene, the physical basis of the poem. That calf also conveys the fresh, primitive response of the two men to the sun; it evokes the frisky, vital movement of fresh language, rather than a staid, bovine, nearly inert response to the world.

"Three" is a poem about translation—translation of our physical experience, translation of our response, and finally, translation of a poem. The sun is speechless; the calf moans; the poet utters his response—and the translator-companion moves toward the moment when he must convey all of this in his own words, his own language.

1986

The Beginning-End of Yiddish

And now? What are you now?
A man on the cold ground—motionless, dumb,
a piece of marble carved by death's candle. A beginning-end.
—Moyshe-Leyb Halpern, "Isaac Leybush Peretz"

If the mark of Yiddish is upon you—not as a language you were born into and shared with a community, but a language you have come to because it carries the seeds of its own mortality, because it possesses the sinuosities of a Jewish diaspora identity— then you feel you have given yourself to a language that specializes in crossing borders.

Kafka once assured an audience of fellow Jews in Prague: "But dread of Yiddish, dread mingled with a certain fundamental distaste, is, after all, understandable, if one has the good will to understand it." Versions of Kafka's Jewish burghers of Prague appear in the novels of Aharon Appelfeld, many of whose characters are repelled by Yiddish, which grates on their cultural aspirations. For them to open up to Yiddish is to disrupt their assured sense of themselves and to touch the grittiness under the surface of bourgeois life. Appelfeld's characters would not approve of what I have done by moving toward Yiddish, taking it into my life, though I too began with all that dread and distancing Kafka speaks of. For me, to have moved toward Yiddish is to have moved toward the troubling sources of poetry.

I have been vivified by Yiddish at the very time that it dwindles away. I can say of Yiddish literature and of myself: in its end is my beginning. And I can feel under that remark the squirm of every dead Yiddish writer (a number of them buried within a stone's throw of my parents' graves in New Jersey). They grimace at such usurpation—grimace and nod stiffly in understanding. The dead have a special way of seeping back into your life.

My attachment to Yiddish is inward—it leads back to poetry,

to the private joys of listening to Yiddish folk music—but not to community, to the rebirth of the language, to the reestablishment of Yiddish culture. Something from the past is privately reanimated and perhaps can be reshaped. I think of the brooding displacement evoked by Expressionist stage designs for Yiddish plays in the Soviet Union, their power to convey an eidetic presence without a center.

The lost center of Yiddish becomes the very place where dispossession turns to possession. Every person who now comes to Yiddish knows what it means to be possessed. It's as if the God of history said to Yiddish, "So far, and no further." But we enter it—a body of language that has stopped growing, though still breathing, still luring. At the same time we can't help indulging the thought, "If there had only been more time—for the sake of all those lives, for the sake of what Yiddish might yet have done for a generation or two in Europe and America." (And I must even confess to the fantasy—"If only Yiddish had held out until the breakup of the Soviet Union and the spontaneous burgeoning of national enclaves." Yiddish instructs you in history.)

But what we have, actually, is the difficult consolation offered in a line by Avrom Sutzkever:

Enough to string pearls for a neck no longer here. . . .

Genug tsu silien perl far a haldz vos iz nishtor mer. . . .

How quietly Sutzkever, that last magician of Yiddish poetry, gets the line to echo itself.

That effort to form a Jewish presence in the diaspora through a Jewish language unattached to a polity and land base is now over and perhaps, as some argue, was doomed to failure. Despite, or because of, the lengthy and often awkward mourning period over Yiddish, I do not think we are yet fully aware of the nature of our loss.

The murder of Yiddish should not blind us to the recognition of how vulnerable it really was, how in the 30s it was already entering its last grand act (the act interrupted by the very destruction of the theater). Just think of it—not one major or even significantly minor Yiddish writer of any renown flourished in Central America, South America, Australia or even in Western Europe. Nor did all those Yiddish schools and Yiddish movements in the diaspora (outside Eastern Europe), nor all those Yiddish camps, choirs, dramatic groups, outings and festivals, college courses, learning seminars, third Seders, summer institutes, lecture programs cultivate one significant Yiddish writer. (Of course, many of those students went on to be successful in many fields, including literary scholarship— and with everlasting affection for Yiddish—but not one important Yiddish writer came out of all that activity.) Roots, roots, roots—but no soil. If you wanted to be a Yiddish writer, that sly God of Jewish history said, you had better be born in Russia, Poland, Lithuania, or the Austro-Hungarian Empire. Now, Yiddish has nowhere to reside but inside of us.

Unless we rework Yiddish into our life as a way of further discovering ourselves—rather than revisiting it like an old stage set—Yiddish remains a mere remnant, an antique interest of great sentimental force yet merely indulgent retrospections. It is then warm to our heart but blank to the sensations of our world, except as mock imitation. Because of history it is impossible for Yiddish to play a revitalizing role in the lives of most people who possess the language; the only thing left is the spur of personal Yiddish stimulation. I was wide-eyed when I read in Benjamin Harshav's keen survey, *The Meaning of Yiddish,* that "it is not the systematic essay but the concatenation of an associative chain that characterizes Yiddish discourse. . . ." Why, I thought, that's exactly how I write. From how many family gatherings did I as a child unknowingly absorb this method, I wondered. How did it get inside me? How did I become "a Yiddish mode of discourse"?

Toward the end of *Remembrance of Things Past,* the narrator confesses, "I had a longing to go the Guermantes party as if in going there I must have been brought nearer to my childhood and to the depths of my memory where my childhood dwelt." Replace "Yiddish" for "Guermantes party" and you have the source of my return to Yiddish—in my case a return that is true possession in the first place. And furthermore, to know now—as I never could imagine about the rag-tag Yiddish of my childhood—that Yiddish could be turned into poetry! I will never get over the thrill of that discovery, as if one discovered long latent powers in oneself. It's like the frog turning into a prince.

The allure of Yiddish poetry for me now is not so much to translate it as to absorb it until it becomes transformed into my own poetry. Yiddish poetry is for me the way into an immigrant past that is closed to me yet that has a transforming power in its very distance. It is my way back to a nearby past that is both a culture in its own right and the unclaimed world of my early years, a past that shimmers with a newness only the past can possess.

Despite my cool attitude toward the nostalgic pull of Yiddish, I'm a part of what I censure. I am often touched by the tug of the response Yiddish can bring about. Never before or since did I receive a note like the one I found tacked by students to my office door after a dean canceled a Yiddish class because of low enrollment. The note, with its frayed edge ripped out of a spiral notebook read: "Prof. Fein, finding out about the cancellation of elem. Yiddish One was very upsetting to all of us. Can you meet with us as soon as possible to consider having the class anyway? (We will be here Thurs. 11:00.) We are desperately interested." What other course would evoke a response like that, such phrasing?

One evening, after I gave a reading of my translations of Yankev Glatshteyn's poetry and the original poems, a man came up to me and said, "When Glatshteyn died I felt all the green leaves had fallen off the tree." But then (as if to embolden the translator), the spirit of Glatshteyn later reappeared, repeating what he once said during an interview, "the Yiddish poem will arrive in the world through English translation." Alongside such painful candor,

Glatshteyn continued to write in the language which he had to write in. (Ghosts of Yiddish poets have variously visited me.)

Despite its lagging vital signs, I sometimes think that we have only begun to see what power Yiddish can have in the culture and art created by American Jews, that the dying power of Yiddish (that "beginning-end") is still speaking to us, not as a vibrant Yiddish culture but as a waning force transformed into the terms of American culture, say the way Ziggy Elman took a klezmer melody and turned it into "And the Angels Sing." We have yet to see a director who knows how to turn the Yiddish film into an American one. The American director Eleanor Antin's version of shtetl life, *The Man Without a World* (1992) is a quirky effort in this direction, even turning some of Roman Vishniac's photographs into moving pictures. My fondest film fantasy is for someone to direct I. B. Singer's *Satan in Goray* on location in Poland, in Yiddish. (I know the character in the novel I want to play.) I imagine some artist (Larry Rivers?) doing for Yiddish proverbs what Pieter Brueghel the Elder did for German proverbs in his 1559 painting, *Proverbs of the Lowlands.*

The appeal and tragedy of Yiddish is that it is a language without a land (*a sprakh ohn a land*); the attraction and burden of modern Hebrew, on the other hand, is that it is the Sacred Tongue attached to a modern nation state. Yiddish speaks to us because it has no national seat. And the very reason it speaks to us is the reason we will lose it. And in losing it, we lose the diaspora language that is also a Jewish language. In that condition it speaks more sympathetically than ever to some. As Yiddish nears the end of its tether, it slips inside of us (a language of private dedication) to reemerge—for some as scholarship, for some as music, dance and theater, and for a few as translation and poetry—which shows how for purposes of intellectual work and of art, one can be tied to "a half-lost and broken past." (I borrow the phrase from C. M. Bowra's description of that great residual poet of the Greek diaspora, Constantine Cavafy.) With both its dark and gleaming side, Yiddish becomes a moon within us. It then reappears as the book of our lives, the book that can only emerge from our affections and our vulnerability. And then I hear in the lines of Moyshe Kulbak from his poem "Vilna," an appeal that is both pensive and vivifying:

> I sit and hear the raw sounds of Yiddish.
> Is that why my blood's racing through my veins?

> *Zits ikh dor un horkh di roye shtim fun yidish.*
> *Un efsher roysht es azoy shtark dos blut in mayne glider?*

"Sounds" in my translation rather than Kulbak's "voice" (*"shtim"*), because what was a full-throated language to Kulbak was to me in childhood a throng of sounds.

1994

What Can Yiddish Mean to an American Poet?

"Late resounds in us what early sounded."
—Theodore Reik, *Jewish Wit*

For so long, Yiddish has thrived on its own demise. It has become its own dybbuk—occupied by the presence of its former self. We can imagine the nature of its appeal lying in the very life of its dissolution—the bracing taste of our mortality.

For me, reaching into Yiddish was also groping inward to a language that I had spurned when younger but that suddenly—or not so suddenly—began to speak to me, or nudge up to me. To come to Yiddish as I did is like having a love affair in middle age with someone known years before but back then rejected as ungainly, embarrassing, and pushy. Now, the sounds and nuances evoke a pleasure I had once never thought possible, just as once I thought that a woman's gray hair would never be alluring. Cynthia Ozick embeds this late embrace with words of longing, "We translate Yiddish with the fury of lost love."

In a sense I did not go into Yiddish, but Yiddish came upon me. It is a specter from childhood; it is a night thought, a visitation of the shadows in the back rooms of shops I couldn't really look into when I was a child. There were indistinct gargles there, hazy movements and figures beyond some chintzy curtain over a doorway. Somewhere in back rooms with remote shelves were one shoe, a deserted bolt of cloth, a mismatched cap and bottle. I can never know what exactly was there but feel again the child's halting curiosity. Sounds, like shapes, lay their hands on him. Whatever it was that shadowed the back rooms of those neighborhood stores, and beyond them to the Galicia, Volhynia, and Bessarabia those bodies came from, I can only know by reading and imagining. And thus every Yiddish word comes from a destroyed and precious region that simultaneously shapes and vanishes as I enter it. How different Yiddish was for the wagon driver (*der bal-agoleb*), the female bathhouse attendant (*di tukerin*), the pampered son-in-law financed so he could continue his religious studies (*an eydem af kest*). For them, Yiddish was merely normal, and therefore, for me, strange.

For some of us, Yiddish might be seen as our orphan-language of early years which squirmed underneath (or alongside) that English we were bound to learn. In our growing up, Yiddish became our relic that we later sought to recover—say the way a poet goes back to claim and refigure early feelings.

If a poet goes back to immigrant experience, the Bible, or Yiddish literature and life for some of his themes, he must first feel that those themes are really his own—not borrowings, approached identities, dutiful attachments, or exhumed exotica. Either you feel the *frisson* or you don't, I mean to say *der tsiter* of Yiddish. The poet must find in those realms the provocations of his moods, the longings of his ignorance, knowing what he has lacked is more important than where he has willed to go. Otherwise, Yiddish is cozily worked up for a delicacy, a celebration, a mere identity.

Robert Pinsky has extrapolated Zishe Landau's famous quip that Yiddish poetry had heretofore been the rhyme department of the Jewish labor movement to mean, in our day, "cleaving for material to the Holocaust, to the Old Testament, or to reminiscences of the immigrant generation." A shrewd admonition this, but if these sources writhe inside of you and are part of your natural turmoil, then the cleaving is genuine, and so the emerging poems will strive to be genuine. If Genesis, Yiddish, Grandmother's mortar and pestle, passageways of Vilna are a commotion inside of you and must be revealed in poems, then the relationship to that material is primal, not a "cultural reach." Like Yeats, a poet might be steeped in his attachments, even maimed by them, yet not narrowed by them. Indeed, in the danger of confinement there also lies a challenge: to be used by that material in a way even the material had not imagined until you came along. I once dreamed that Lionel Trilling strolled with me in the woods behind the college where I used to teach. Avuncularly, he warned me not to become too narrow by studying

Yiddish. I told him that Yiddish is my "reconsidered passion." "Hmmm," his sinus intoned at the allusion to Eliot, and we walked further into the woods.

One day, when I was still teaching, it dawned on me that Nathaniel Hawthorne, Henry Adams and Robert Lowell had all visited their New England-family past in order to write some of their best work. They weren't after "roots," by which I mean some self-satisfying connection to the family past, some affirmation of self through historical-familial-religious and ethnicky ties. But they were scouring their true material, which included their ambivalence about the past which molded them. By going back to Puritan judges, former Presidents, Indian killers and Civil War heroes, they were reaching deeply into themselves, their own condition emerging from family lives, family memory, from the past that obsessed them. The risks of such returns (I should prefer to think of it as re-immersion) are the obvious ones of sentimentality, self-congratulations, facile tribal affirmations, folksy rejections of modernity and, perhaps worst of all, neat "identity." But there are also arduous and soul-shaking discoveries in such a re-immersion, real confrontations with oneself, as, say, Lowell's presence in *Lord Weary's Castle* as a descendant of Indian killers who is himself a conscientious objector to World War II, and yet a son who knocks down his own father during a quarrel—the recoil in Lowell's own sense of himself.

Suddenly seeing these New England writers in their ravel of family-national material made me feel closer to them than ever before, and not only because of that tangle of hard-won insights, but also because of the *process* of their inquiries, their discoveries—their entry into that past because of who they were in the present. They had suddenly become more than writers whose work I taught, even more than writers I admired, but writers whose process became mine as well. And in that sense we had all become contemporaries. Despite obvious differences, it was as if what they had gone through in their own ways was what I was now experiencing in my own terms. I had never felt so close to them before. We had all become—

dare I include myself?—part of an American procedure—part of a still unfolding act—and I had somehow slipped myself in. Or maybe a fairer way of putting it is that I could envision myself at another part of a frequency band. I too had gone back to what shaped me; with all of my compulsions I could conjure or summon up relatives. And like the Lowell in *Life Studies,* I had also managed to expand my family to include writers I had never met, writers I admired (even those who had given me and my people pain), and in some way they intersected the world of my parents, uncles and aunts, *almost, as if . . .* even Henry Adams might grasp "snarling weird Yiddish": *hypokrit leyener, mayn glaykher, mayn bruder.*

While reading Section XII of Seamus Heaney's *Station Island,* where James Joyce returns to visit the poet (or his persona), I felt ghost-envy. Why couldn't a poet visit me, I thought. I knew it wouldn't be Joyce. And then shortly after, Yankev Glatshteyn visited me. I knew in which booth in which coffee shop on East 86th Street in New York Glatshteyn visited me. I was facing the back. He had come in from the street and before I knew it slid in opposite me. Then, weeks and months later, three other Yiddish poets visited me, also speaking poems. (Did I break the bank with Heaney's poem?) It's visitations like these that feed my chimera (*mayn kapriz*) that I am the last Yiddish poet who, however, writes in English. ("Lying is lovely if we choose it," poses Rahel Varnhagen, "and is an important component of our freedom.") I think those visitations are over (though you never know), and I have gone on to other subjects. But such revenants help you find a voice, as your anxieties and theirs converge. Out of their death they give you breathing room. At the same time, through them, you make contact with that Yiddish world they know in their bones. I feel as if those ghosts gave me access to their poems spoken on their brief return.

It has taken me so long to get to Yiddish (and from there to my own poetry). I read and read Whitman without understanding:

O I have been dilatory and dumb,
I should have made my way straight to you long ago,
I should have blabb'd nothing but you, I should have
        chanted nothing but you.
("To You")

To turn to poetry when you're over fifty is to feel you've picked up a task, a part of yourself, long ago put aside, and you chance the illusion of finding, as Y. Y. Troonk, the great Yiddish memoirist turned poet, put it, the last rhythms of your life in the rhythm of a poem. You write out of the confusion and spoilage of your life and hope something will cohere, will be a reliable witness.

I feel exhilarated and fraudulent in my possession of Yiddish. It's as if Yiddish poets would come back and say to me, "Use us as you will—we too were poets—we know how it works—but just remember, that language and culture really *was* ours. We argued with it as you cannot; we can feel its loss as you cannot—you thief, you exploiter, you Yiddish grabber, your legitimacy, your very inspiration, based on the death of our tongue! What *can* Yiddish mean to you? You think we were only there for your sake? But go . . . go. Write. Use us . . . use us." My only self-defense could be the poems I made, including those in which these ghosts cozy up, instruct, reprove and keep their distance once again.

I put on the clothing and become the heir—the usurper out of the destruction. There is not a single Yiddish word that does not quiver inside of me as something that I've tried to make mine but really belongs to another. My middle name is Jacob. I've schemed myself into a legacy.

If I had to choose an image for Yiddish now, it comes at the end of Mani-Leyb's sonnet, "A Plum." (Poets like to write about plums because they look like purple gifts that might have come from China.) The poet plucked a plum, bit into it, wetting his fingers. So as not to lose any of the juice he carried the fruit in both hands, like cradling a cup of wine,

and gently raised it
to his wife's lips. Lovingly, she

thanked him and gnawed
the plum in his hands down
to skin and pit and speckled pulp.

What compelled me to translate the poem, I think, is that final image, which conveys to me the condition of Yiddish. The poem is not only a metaphor of sex but also about language used up yet possessed in its ruin, in its bits and pieces, and for all of that savored by the wife, who is grateful for receiving it. Attractive, bitten remnants remain—the shiny leftovers.

We were denied more folksongs and the people who would sing them. We were denied another generation or two of writers steeped in both Yiddish and western culture, writers who knew Flaubert and James as well as they knew Dovid Bergelson; Roethke and Hardy as well as Itsik Manger; Edmund Wilson as well as Shmuel Niger, but who, most of all, felt the folk motifs of Yiddish (women's religious literature; folk songs; sayings) and could play those sources off western skepticism through the end of the twentieth century. The handwriting on the wall would have driven the last generation or two of Yiddish writers to touch their materials with new life before the generations came who would really be out of touch. What wonders we would have had. History churned elsewhere. (Still, I imagine a young Yiddish writer in the 50s, just out of college, sitting on a bench in Washington Square Park, reading *Partisan Review*, his Yiddish stirred up.)

If the shifty Jewish God came to me and said, "Look here, Fein, Yiddish will survive and expand—we're agreed to that up here—but on only one condition, that you lay down your life for it," I hope that I would have the courage to make the deal, stipulating one condition myself: that before I go I write a folksong in Yiddish that people will sing for centuries even though they might not know who wrote it. It would be like inventing proverbs—one then had a permanent stake in the language. Yiddish can up the ante of your life.

Once having learned Yiddish I had to bring the poetry of Yankev Glatshteyn over into English. I receive more than I could give. Reaching into him I reached into myself. I could feel his mark on me. I think of my relationship to Glatshteyn in the way William Rossetti described Dante Gabriel Rossetti's relationship to his translations *Dante and His Circle*: "If he had not undertaken the translations, and had not given them the development they here assume, some substantial traits in his own poetry would be less intelligibly marked and less securely recognizable."

Nearing the end of my translations of Glatshteyn I spent six months in Berlin, and while walking its streets during the late afternoons in January shortly after I arrived, I felt a poem coming to me, like the darkening air of Berlin entering my pores. Unaware of it at the time, I now suspect that Glatshteyn's "music of fear" which he achieved in his foreboding Holocaust poem "Wagons" seeped into my own work:

> It gets dark early in Berlin,
> by four dusk comes creeping in.
> At first a gauzy wane,
> whose beige shades lengthen
> and thicken to a tawny smear.
> Then a dun vapor
> begins to curdle and fissure
> till a gray grit sweeps the air.
> Finally, sallow lights turn
> brown streets browner.
> In the afternoons trains grow full,
> as if everyone knew
> it gets dark early in Berlin,
> by four dusk comes creeping in.

The poem is called "January in Berlin" (from *Kafka's Ear*). I might have called it "Homage to Glatshteyn."

Yiddish can speak to us at that point where articulation passes into intonation, the point, as William Hazlitt noted, where poetry begins. And that occurs when the Yiddish past stirs within us as a present. It's not the eternity of Yiddish we want to hear about, but the immediacy of its demise that shines like the fruit the wife eats for all it is worth.

1996

Waiting for Yiddish

When I was a child, Yiddish was awkwardly present in my ear, a set of invasive sounds claiming me beyond comprehension or will—one of those magnified impressions from the adult world one could neither escape nor comprehend. To have come back to the language in middle age (if it is a return and not a discovery in the first place) is like approaching one's past anew. This possession is a re-creation.

There's a striking passage in II Kings (13:20-21) about the prophet Elisha:

> Then Elisha died and was buried.
>
> Year by year Moabite raiders used to invade the land. Once some men were burying a dead man when they caught sight of the raiders. They threw the body into the grave of Elisha and made off; when the body touched the prophet's bones, the man came to life and rose to his feet.

Let me explicate. The Moabite raiders are the attractions of Western culture. The body is Yiddish. Elisha is the need for something vital within you. The man come alive is the rebirth of Yiddish within an American poet who still traffics with those raiders whose very invasion prompted the hasty burial and the unexpected rebirth.

In my relationship to Eastern European Jewish culture and Yiddish, I am authentically inauthentic. In my inability to be truly of that culture, yet in that very process of discontinuity and fracture to make it mine, is the condition of my life and many of my poems. What I once spurned or mocked, or felt uncomfortably invading me when young, came, in time, to be among the deepest sources of my work.

Yiddish has been for me a way of entering that part of myself I had feared to enter, yet, once having entered, found to be my true place. For a poet, this return to the parts of himself he previously rejected is one of the most important journeys he can make, especially when that return includes an effort to recover the sounds of a language barely comprehended even as they were sealed into childhood. Like the confusions of childhood, the sounds of Yiddish made their mark, vivid and incomprehensible. Kafka speaks of "the tangle of Yiddish." Yiddish has been for me like the gesture of every poem—retrieve, retrieve, *krigtsurik, krigtsurik.*

I have never quite been able to shake off my sense of myself as a transgressor, a usurper, in the world of Yiddish. I take some encouragement from the words of the poet Richard Hugo, who wrote in his idiosyncratic and spirited book about poetry, *The Triggering Town,* "It is narcissistic, vain, egotistical, selfish and hateful to assume emotional ownership of a town or a world. It is also essential." Several times, long-dead Yiddish writers have come to me and told me they understand my need to usurp their worlds, and if that's what it takes for me to get close to them and for them to feel new stirrings, they accede and give me the right of way despite their regret at not being here on their own terms. I feel as if the literary critic A. Tabachnik prepared the way for my reading and translating Yiddish when he bemoaned the demise of Yiddish culture and sighed that Yiddish poetry is "perhaps our only remaining bit of consolation." Maybe that's why those dead Yiddish poets sanction me. They are my guides, whose very dwellings I seek.

Yiddish haunts me because it is about death-in-life, about memory that lingers while the world that was the basis of that memory has been extinguished, or nearly so. Yiddish creates in the midst of its own end—that seems to be its specialty—just as it was given to me to come to poetry in middle age. (It's as if the urgent, late development of Yiddish literature is internalized in me.) Somehow, because Yiddish did not have world enough and time, it has become for me a seedbed, some essential domain, where I once feared to grow but that I must now make part of my life, turn into poems.

I would like to lie down in the pool of Yiddish and have the language seep into me and then exude from me as part of my own poems in English. I would then feel I had arrived where I alone was meant to go—to turn my sense of Yiddish into an English poem. Thus, bringing the poetry of Yankev Glatshteyn over into English initiated within me "the crystallization of the poet's own personality" (his phrase). Aaron Tseytlin, the Yiddish poet, once asked, "Who needs a poem . . . and in Yiddish no less?" *Ver darf a lid—un nokh dertsu af yidish?* I do. I will never get over the thrill that Yiddish can be turned into poetry.

I always suspect that the Yiddish speakers I heard as a child felt they weren't really speaking a language—certainly not a language like English, French, or German, nationhoods you could point to on a map—but some tribal tongue, *our* way of talking. And that speech, that tribalism, entered me—beyond my desire, beyond my pleasure—creating bonds and associations, discomforts and confusions I could appreciate and draw on only decades and decades later. It's as if one has a childhood in order to recall it and write about it half a century later, and it seems all the more real because of its late generation.

The sounds of undecipherable experience, Yiddish was like a poem that entered me but that I didn't understand, waiting for me to grasp it. But it was also, and no less significantly, distressing and embarrassing. There was something about Yiddish that made me squirm—not only the language itself but some of its speakers. I remember seeing the slapstick face of the comedian Menashe Skulnik on posters advertising Yiddish films. To my childish fears the bony-comic clang of his last name and the old world smirch of his first name combined with his goggle-eyed, shit-eating smile and thick-lipped face to make for a kind of Yiddish Stepin Fetchit. And back then, I hoped that none of him would rub off on me. Yiddish got inside of me in more ways than one, and it was all there in the act of retrieval when I returned to Yiddish in adulthood. Yiddish has brought me to the deep place.*

As a kid I used to titter over such Yiddish words as *fokhn* (to

---

*Some five decades after my revulsion at that name, I savored the lyrical plaint of "Menashe, Menashe" in a Yiddish folk song rendered by the cantorial-operatic voice of Mikhail Alexandrovitch.

fan) and *shitn* (to pour or strew). Later on, when I was grappling to make Yiddish my own, I'd wince at Borscht Belt jokes and nightclub routines and songs that played on such crude Yiddish-English *double entendres.* I then felt sorrow that Yiddish had to suffer such scorn, and I was annoyed with the performers who traded on such crass puns, ignoring the real sarcastic and lewd powers of Yiddish. But in my adult disapproval I knew that I was annoyed not only with the philistine comedians but also with myself, because I had once been among them. Me, the Saint Paul of Yiddish!

Now, I wanted so much from Yiddish. I long wanted the presence of Yiddish in my poetry as something more than a letter, a phrase, an occasional line, as something more than a fleeting presence. Whereas in my translations of Glatshteyn's poetry the two languages worked out their relationship on facing pages (two wings of a butterfly, as a friend of mine put it), I wanted a play between the two languages in the same poem. Shortly after writing a poem about being visited by the ghost of Glatshteyn, I heard Prokofiev's "Overture on Hebrew Themes," and listening to the piece opened the door for me. He used the melodies of Yiddish folksongs for his own purposes, and so I wanted to do something comparable. I fancied a concurrent English and Yiddish poem. Not some macaronic freak, but a poem in which the two languages needed to play off one another. And so I wrote a poem of couplets as takeoff from Prokofiev's piece, in which the two languages shadow one another, like overlapping yet independent moons.

> Jew seeps from all instruments, not just the fiddle.
> *Nit nur funem fidl, nur fun ale keylim krikht aroys dos yidl.*

Franz Rosenzweig has meditated on the condition of the Jew, whose Jewishness resides in a realm of desire and delay: "In Judaism, man is always a remnant—somehow or other. Somehow or other, he is always something left over, an inner being whose husk has been seized upon and swept away by the current of the world, while he himself, that is to say what remained of him, stands on the shore. Something within him is waiting. And he has something within himself. He may give different names to what he is waiting for, and to what is inside himself. Often he will not be able to find any name for it at all. But he has the feeling that both this having and this waiting are intimately bound up with each other."

In my case it was simply that I was granted Yiddish, and the East European Jewish mood, and its Brooklyn waning version, and I waited, without my knowing it, for them to stir within me.

And in time I entered a new condition, beautifully voiced to me by my friend Sholem Beinfeld, who said (in Yiddish) one day as we were strolling along Ware St. in Cambridge, "I am a diaspora Jew, not in exile from Zion but from the pre-war world of East European Jewry."

1999

Jew, Poet

"What have I in common with Jews? I have hardly anything in common with myself and should stand very quietly in a corner, content that I can breathe."
—Kafka, *Diaries*

It is not difficult to imagine Manasseh (one of the sons of Joseph) reading and underlining that passage from the *Diaries*. Kafka's remark evinces one of the ways a Jew estranged from Judaism becomes a Jew. Kafka knew how one can eat the matzah, drink the wine, say the blessings, yet share something with the wicked son. And Kafka knew this condition not only in his intellect but in his nervous system, which became for him *a way of knowing.*

Within the skepticism, insecurity—that nescient world so deep in Kafka's work—lies a sense of missing sacredness, and he can evoke that vacancy in startling ways. In *Letter to His Father*, Kafka describes his boyhood boredom when he went to synagogue, though he tried his best

> to enjoy the few little bits of variety there were,
> as for instance when the Ark of the Covenant was
> opened, which always reminded me of the shooting
> galleries where a cupboard door would open in the
> same way whenever one hit a bull's eye; except
> that there something interesting always came out and
> here it was always just the same old dolls with heads.

The humor, the leap, the daring, the insistence on the truth of his feelings are spirited impieties. The knobby tops of the scroll handles bare Kafka's desire for a religious experience from religion as deep and provoking as a child's response to his world. Kafka was doing in his way what any writer must do for himself—in his case creating out of the complex material that made him son and Jew.

I am the kind of Jew for whom the title *Genesis* has more

resonance than the title *B'reyshis*. I am the kind of Jew who, early on, became attached to the King James translation of the Bible, and then, later on, in adulthood, to the Yiddish translation by Yehoash, "a new original," in the words of Glatshteyn. In essence, then, I'm a Bible Jew and a Yiddish Jew, and like Daniel in the court of Nebuchadnezzar one instructed in the language and literature of the Chaldeans. If I'm a Jewish poet—parlous term—it's because inside of me is a curious mix of these elements, a mix that compulsively enters my work; no, I would say at times determines it. I am uncomfortable with the idea of being a Jewish poet. Rather, I feel, to paraphrase what Chagall said about himself, if I were not Jewish I would not be a poet, or at least I would not write the way I do. But I'm not a Jewish poet.

The possession of Yiddish in middle age was crucial to my sense of myself as a Jew and a poet. Yiddish is a language I never knew, then forgot. Then learned. In a strange way, it opened me up to what I had spurned or failed to see about myself. Yiddish, for me, I sometimes think, is what the occult was to Yeats: irrelevant to practical life, yet out of its grip I make poems, keep my tie to underground life, to the dead who once inhabited the language, to the ghosts of my own past. Yiddish is the ur-language in which my poems yearn to be written, perhaps in which they are written before they come to English. Rilke says somewhere that every poem is a translation.

R. P. Blackmur, in his essay on Emily Dickinson, speculates that perhaps the deepest problem in poetics is "How much does a poet look to words to supply what is put down and how much to notate what was within the self prior to the words?" For me, "prior to the words" is this indwelling of Yiddish which often (though, thank God, not always) leads me to my poems.

How does that life of Jewish Eastern Europe inhabit those of us who were born in Brooklyn? How does it make its way into our poems? That chord was struck by Charles Reznikoff in a poem he wrote when I was three years old:

The dust of this Russia,
breathed these many years,
is stored in my bones,
stains the skull and cortex of my brain—
the chameleon in us
that willy-nilly
takes the color where we lie.
("In Memoriam")

Some poets and critics are fond of talking about the breath of a line of verse. Just as important is the breathing done *before* the line is written. I cherish Muriel Rukeyser's remark that Whitman "remembered his body as other poets of his time remembered English verse." Yiddish, deep inside of me, came to be the matter that I rejected and then needed most of all. When a poet starts tapping his dangerous material he will find his true rhythms. A psychotherapist once told me he could tell a patient was reaching that point because the rhythms of his voice would change.

The details of the Brooklyn-Jewish world I employ in my poems have less to do with social reality than with the compulsions and distortions of memory, with the needs of invention. In other words, the poems are not bins or valises of Jewish-American material as much as they are obsessions with childhood memories (real or invented), with the conjured matrices of a world that shaped me. My Brooklyn is a confabulation. (I come from a part of Brooklyn so Jewish that I thought even the fire hydrants were circumcised.)

Paul Goodman once paraphrased a remark of Goethe's that "he did not write from his experience but tended to experience what was in him to write." It feels like that even when you are drawing from "real experience." It's that obsession, that interweaving, not the sheer recall or social fact or physical element, that is the heart of the matter. I long to write poems whose factual details change into something other than themselves, as if only thereby do poems exert their deepest selves, which Kafka was getting at when he spoke of "arriving at that freedom of true description which releases one foot from the experienced." Poetry lies in the spell of the ordinary. I want poems that are as clear and mysterious as toes, instep, veins, ankle, and leg hair in a foot of water offshore. Yet I don't mean something as patent and routine as symbolism, but something simpler and deeper—the way the world is a bounty of sense impressions the mind is continually transposing to its own realms.

Childhood is a good place for a poet to return to. Not because of its supposed innocence, but because a child is dominated by magnified impressions he can neither escape nor comprehend. Conjured scenes of childhood memory have a rich oppression about them. Children do not yet know of ideologies, which subsume impressions, and thus they are vulnerable to experiences and images that they cannot shape to preconceptions. In their vulnerability, their nakedness—their terror or joy or puzzlement in the act of reception—lies the connection between childhood and the impulse to poetry, which the adult mind then forges with its own abilities and needs. In returning to that world of remembered detail—a world where Yiddish, childhood memory, and nuances of Jewish-American are like dead relatives returning to long-abandoned living rooms— my poems are needful distortions. The essence of such returns and re-creations is conveyed in a question the Soviet painter El Lissitzky put to himself while looking for signs of earlier Jewish art in Russia, "Isn't that a rabbinic face on the lion's head in the zodiac painting in the Mohilev synagogue?"

The poet achieves his triumph, when he does, through that transformation of the material itself. Strangely enough, that can occur when the subject relinquishes itself to its inherent rhythms, so to speak. About "Wagons," his great poem anticipating the Holocaust, Yankev Glatshteyn had said that he "kept on looking for the music of fear in the poem." In Glatshteyn's case the fear of a generation is conveyed like an aura hovering over the poem, like a shadow of the yet-to-come (his ways of putting it). In this case his material found its sounds from inside of itself, revealed not as idea or commentary, but in the very composition of terror. Here are the

66

opening lines of his poem, first in my translation, then the original:

Night falls. Forlorn wagons—
looming, quiet—from afar.
The doors are open wide,
but no one waits to welcome them.
Quiet village, bells of silence.
Each obedient blade of grass
bends beneath the kindled coolness.

Mit shtile tseykhns fun vayt
kumen on farnakht troyerike vegener.
S'shteyen oyfgepralt tirn,
nor inergets vart nisht keyn bagegener.
S'dorf iz ruik, s'klingen glokn fun shtilkeyt.
S'beygt zikh gehorkhik yeder grezl
unter tsetsundener kilkeyt.

The contractions, the delay of nominatives, the alliteration that oddly stresses quietness—all have the effect of almost nullifying the subjects. (My translation couldn't equal the Yiddish.) A poet's rhythms are what happens when he meets his true material, when he's obsessed by it. In his poem Glatshteyn discovered the measures of diminution.

I translate Yiddish poetry as if I'm rising out of Yiddish, this language once evaded that then spoke to me as my task. I have my private encounters with Yiddish. When I read poetry in English I know (somewhere inside me) that I am part of a community of readers. When reading Yiddish poetry I feel I am entirely alone, the only one reading the poem, perhaps the last reader of the poem. This isolation strangely invigorates me, like the solitude out of which poems come. My affection is spurred by loss, as if the body of Yiddish poetry lives its death inside of me. "It is, finally, my beautiful lover, and I hope to die at its feet." So said Lamed Shapiro, the short story writer, of the Yiddish language. Translating Yiddish poetry can be a way of reconfiguring my own poetry, or my sense of English poetry. At the end of Anna Margolin's poem "She with the cold, marble breasts..."—most of which is inscribed on her tombstone—I insinuate a difference between her last lines and the last lines of Yeats's "Under Ben Bulben," on his tombstone:

> Cast a cold eye
> On life, on death.
> Horseman, pass by!

Margolin's poem ends:

> Here she lies, broken and alone.
> All shame has left her body.
> Passerby—look, have pity
> and say nothing.

My lines part from Margolin's Yiddish in only one essential way, and that is my insertion of the word "look." I wanted her "look, have pity" to argue with Yeats's "Cast a cold eye." Thus I relate—not without tension or differences—a Yiddish poet and an Irish one. Arcane and extravagant as this might sound, I wanted, through my translation of Margolin's next-to-last line, to tell Yeats that his lines bother me (even though he wrote some uncanny poems when he cultivated a cold passion).

To get to a poem of my own by way of a Yiddish poem is important for me and is, no doubt, another example—at the ground level of language—of how I am a diaspora poet. Manasseh and Orpah (the daughter-in-law who does not go with Naomi) speak two of my poems because, in part, I want biblical characters—like those in Itzik Manger's midrash poems—to come out of a world that I know or imagine. Manger's poems opened a way for me to write about biblical characters. I wanted those figures who rarely or never speak in the Bible to speak now, to utter their troubled sense of being Jewish. I wanted a new sense of their lives—in the Bible, in my life, in my sense of God, and thus those members of my internal religious household could live with me in acute ways.

It is always the task of the poet to give speech where there wasn't speech before. In finding a voice (for himself and for the people in his poems), the poet achieves a moral purpose that is consonant with the integrity of poetry itself. This is another way of saying that in achieving his style the poet achieves his deepest end because the style (the way the poem speaks) is one with his human concerns. That is why poems resist efforts to peel off ideas from their very texture.

I doubt that T. S. Eliot had Yiddish poets in mind when he wrote "Tradition and the Individual Talent," though I think of those poets when I read the passage:

> we shall often find that not only the best, but the most
> individual parts of his [a poet's] work may be those in
> which the dead poets, his ancestors, assert their
> immortality most vigorously.

Those dead Yiddish poets and I keep up a conversation.

Rilke called Russia "the homeland of my instinctual being." So I feel about Yiddish, a language, part of a way of life, though not a land. For it was through Yiddish—those sounds of my instinctual being I once fled—that I came back to the writing of poetry. This is an obsession I have written about, as if the ancient mariner was himself the wedding guest at the door.

2002

The Navel of the Bialy: Yiddish Poetry and the Needs of a Translator

"the tangle of Yiddish"
—Franz Kafka

Twice while I was riding on Amtrak from Boston to New York, the specters of Yiddish poets appeared to me. Poems emerged from their generative visits. The first time I was reading the passage of Seamus Heaney's *Station Island* when a figure, most likely James Joyce, visits the poet and encourages and advises him. I found myself jealous. I wished some poet would so visit me, though I didn't think he would be an Irish poet. And before I got to New York, I sensed the tutelary spirit of the Yiddish poet who has meant the most to me, and I had notes toward what would become the poem "Yankev Glatshteyn Visits Me in the Coffee Shop," during which he encourages me to write my own poems and to translate Yiddish poetry.

The second time, when I was going down to give a reading of my translations of Yiddish poetry, I was reading the letters of Kafka, and feeling sleepy I closed the book, left it in my lap, and fitfully napped for an hour or so, opening up my eyes when I heard the conductor call out, "New Haven next." I looked out the window and saw a woman walking a large dog along the edge of the woods. Her dog stopped and looked at the train. It had a gleaming coat of dark sorrel and was perhaps no more than ten feet away. A little later on, still looking at the woods, I thought I saw Yiddish poets (about five or six of them) come out toward the clearing between the woods and the tracks. They were cloaked figures, thin and fleeting versions of Rodin's Balzac. They gathered for a moment at the dark edge of the woods, staring at the train passing by, at the passengers passing by. Yet, somehow, they followed the train as it moved. Sometimes they would scurry back into the woods. Sometimes it seemed they came out from behind the trees and sometimes it seemed they came out from within the trees. They didn't say anything or gesture, just looked—now standing closer, now farther away—in their odd flurry between train and woods. And then I thought I heard them say to me—in English as I recall—"We give you our voices. Read our poetry so we will still be alive. We give you the power to read us." As it worked out, they had appeared collectively to give me a poem, "Yiddish Poets Speak to Me from the Grave," in which they offer encouragement and advice, as if they know me better than I know myself. Some of what they said became lines in the poem. On more recent trips to New York, these poets haven't appeared. The two times these Yiddish poets did appear I was sitting on the right side of the train, from where I could watch the woods up close, glimpsing the distant Atlantic beyond the windows on the other side.

Translations and my own poems are the closest I can get to these poets. If only I could write Yiddish poems (which I do once in a blue moon, with the help of friends who really know the language), I wouldn't have to translate these poets; I would be one of them. But since I don't live in their neck of the woods, I absorb their poems as best I can, finding that some secrete into English—either as translations, or as poems of my own. This is a necessary process for me.

A. E. Housman uses that word *secretion* in one of the most generant remarks I have ever read about the writing of poetry: "If I were obliged not to define poetry, but to name the class of things to which it belongs, I should call it a secretion; whether a natural secretion, like turpentine in the fir, or a morbid secretion, like the pearl in the oyster." There is a curious process of parturient receptivity that seems inherent in the making of poems, curious because it is both passive and active. Housman's emanant metaphor also summons up for me the remark of the well-known translator of Yiddish poetry and fiction, Leonard Wolf, that when we teach Yiddish literature "we are showing students the shell in which a pearl once grew." Still and all, I have this persistent sense that Yiddish poems have long been developing and waiting for me—for me to read them, to translate them, and even to transform them into my own poems.

Indeed, it's precisely because that pearl will no longer grow in that shell that I am attached to it, as if some sand of me has evolved in the same shell after the pearl attained *its* formation.

Just as Jacob followed on the heels of Esau, I wrote a poem of my own after translating H. Leivick's "Here Lives the Jewish People," using the same title. While Leivick imaginatively entered the Lower East Side Jewish world he knew as an immigrant to New York around 1914, I wanted to re-enter the Brooklyn middle class world that stamped itself on me when I was growing up—

> foods yield
> Plonsk-odors that penetrate petals on oilcloth
> and grain the kitchen's bright linoleum . . . .

Later on, the poem conjures up my childhood purchases from the local Jewish bakeries (there were three within five blocks of our apartment),

> Yiddish speaking from the navel of a bialy . . . .

Although Yiddish and childhood in my poetry is more a matter of fabrication that what "actually happened," my compulsion to write my own poetry (and to translate Yiddish poetry) grows out of those early sense impressions. They're eidetic for me, re-shaped during the process of making poems. Yet sometimes, in that process, the right image, for whatever reasons, holds back. Take that passage

> Yiddish speaking from the navel of a bialy . . . .

In version after version of the poem (even into the first set of proofs of the book in which it appears), it was not a bialy but a kaiser roll. Not *too* bad—I could see the triangular seeded folds meeting to form a tiny navel-like center. And I was taken with the incongruity of

72

"Yiddish" and "kaiser," their proposing a stimulating tension between the kindred language of my borough and the title of the German "Caesar." Yet all along I felt that "kaiser roll" wasn't quite right, and only when I was writing this essay did "bialy" come to me—with its navel that really is a belly-button-like crater. The bialy really has a *pupik,* a redolent word (often comic) that even people who have a smattering of Yiddish are familiar with. How could that pronounced navel of the *bialy* have escaped me? Why did it come only when I sat down to write these words about translating Yiddish? Could my reliance on that provocative tension between "Yiddish" and "kaiser" have so seduced me that I couldn't see the umbilicus of that Jewish roll? Did my yielding to rhetorical effect eclipse the most telling image, and one closer to home? Was it the writing of prose that brought me back to the apt concavity? I secretly suspect that *kaiser* came to the fore and scared away *bialy* because even now I can still see myself holding off from entering that early Yiddish world of mine, in this case opting for crafty linguistic and cultural tensions over those actual bakeries of childhood. It's as if every entry into a Yiddish poem is a little drama of my return to that tribal language of childhood, vis-à-vis my engagement with the world of English, which possessed a cluster of sophistications and enticements I long thought put Yiddish to shame. One of the reasons I was attracted to Leivick's poem "Here Lives the Jewish People" is that it is in part a tense correspondence between himself as an adult-immigrant in New York and as a child in Eastern Europe.

Leivick made out of his walking through the streets of the Jewish Lower East Side a visionary poem that also goes back to his childhood obsession with human suffering, and, implicitly, back to his own pain as a political prisoner in Czarist Russia, and to his lifelong inability to comprehend human suffering, even as he senses something revelatory in it. (There is a striking Christian or Dostoyevskian mood of grief fostering redemption, or transformation, in Leivick, and in this regard he is closer to Bernard Malamud than he is to any of his fellow Yiddish poets. Just as Chagall draws near a Jewish-Christology in his paintings of the crucifixion, Leivick tenders a deliverance-through-suffering conception associated with Christianity. Both Chagall and Leivick are pushing the envelope of their Jewish materials.)

Leivick's details of city life culminate in a vision of human suffering, yet his obsessive failure to penetrate that suffering, to understand its pervasiveness in the scheme of things, drives him to further poems, further intensities. I do not know if Leivick ever read Keats's letters, but he would have been taken by one of the most well-known passages in them: "Do you not see how necessary a World of Pains and troubles is to school an Intelligence and make it a soul?" *Why* should this be so, and *how* you enter that schooling, and *why* it is attractive haunted Leivick's entire life. He also suggests that children—unarmored in systems of thought, in ideological rationalizations of all sorts—are closest to human suffering, and thereby to poetry. Leivick's "Here Lives the Jewish People" is an effort to penetrate that suffering—to keep one's life in touch with the disrepair of the world—and therein lies that tenor, or should I say terror, we sense in his poetry, which is often drawn from his memories of childhood. Specifically, in this poem, a cripple he remembers by name from his younger years in a shtetl reappears in the form of a cripple on the Lower East Side. These two figures merge for him in image and puzzlement. Leivick's vision, in the optical sense, is part of his vision in the prophetic sense: The moment is a coda at the end of a working day:

> The life in the towered city
> fades into shades of yellow-gray
> and on the streets of the Jewish East Side
> the yellow-grayness turns more yellow, gray.
> Step by step, the men with the long dresses—
> for girls, for the ladies—disappear around corners;
> and an old woman carries a sick bird,
> fortune-telling cards filling the box in the cage.
> And here's the blind cripple wheeling home

through the streets cleared of pushcarts and stalls.
Longing stirs in me. I follow
the hard-peaked shoulders of the cripple
(Luria was his name).
The approach, the entrance to his den lie in wait for me,
and then I'm stabbed by the stare of a widening eye
fixed in his back between the shoulders.

It is as if the universe itself assaults the pitiful regard of the onlooker. Images grip, but also rebuff, and Leivick cannot fully penetrate the suffering of another, or an explanation. The title, *"Dor voynt dos yidishe folk"* ("Here Lives the Jewish People") becomes at the end of the poem *"Dor shloft dos yidishe folk"* ("Here sleeps the Jewish people"). In this poem Leivick moves from the crowd and rush and noise of the Lower East Side to the realm of disconcerted vision—a dream-like perplexity. We're caught in the wonder and wariness that Leivick imparts in that closing chimerical image as that eye (almost a disembodied creature) seems to look right through him, and he recoils, as the object of his pity stares back at him—the witness becoming the witnessed. The onlooker is himself looked upon by some eye—visionary and appalling. The starer is outstared by the universe his pity seeks to penetrate. The universe sees his pity, but exists somewhere beyond it. I think this is the kind of poetry the prophets would write if they were alive now—revelation unrevealing of a moral center, yet intensifying the visionary's embodiment of the world.

Reading and re-reading Leivick's poem and even while translating it, I did not entirely understand it, even as I possessed it, or it me. That alone may be a reason to translate a poem. The task of translation induces the most intensive act of reading, during which, for example, punctuation can take on an almost physical weight. Though translation brought me closer to it, the poem can still puzzle me or squiggle out of my grasp, often to reconstitute itself into further understanding as I return to it again and again. I have grown into the poem as I have taken it into me. I wonder if it would have become as intimate if I had not translated it. Is translation the higher reading, the truest possession of the poem? I was taken by Leivick's vision, and that's what I had to be loyal to even as it was irregularly clarifying itself to me;* and further, loyal enough, I came up with a poem of my own, with the same title. And thus Leivick's poem enabled me to find, or make, a comparable, though not equivalent, world. In other words, no pushcarts, no fortune tellers and hawkers of dresses on the streets, no paraphernalia of the Jewish Lower East Side, certainly not even an equivalent vision of suffering that so gripped Leivick. Yet his poem could be a tutelary presence for me, and out of it I could write my own poem. The value of Leivick's poem is his need to enter that New York immigrant Jewish world he knew so well and to make out of his poem an experience, not merely a description of that world. Encouraged by Whitman not only to write free verse but to try to penetrate what was happening on the streets, what Leivick finally achieves is description as revelation. I, with only comestible powers, tried to enter that vein.

> Yiddish speaking from the navel of a bialy . . .

Perhaps I can put the connection between Leivick's poem and my own a bit differently than I have heretofore. After translating "Here Lives the Jewish People" my own poem came out as a kind of afterbirth that I shaped into a life of its own. And that alone would warrant the passage from "Out of the Cradle Endlessly Rocking" that I used as an epigraph to my collection of translations of Yiddish poetry, *With Everything We've Got:*

> Listen'd to keep, to sing, now translating the notes,
> Following you my brother.

*Even as I was writing this essay, I realized that I had to change that third from the last line in the passage I quoted, from "I'm lured by the approach—the entrance to his den" to "The approach, the entrance to his den lie in wait for me," as I grasped, better than before, the impending terror of that line.

As I have said, I do not have an elective but an obsessive affinity with Yiddish poets. I wonder if I am compelled to translate Yiddish poetry and to write about my connection to Yiddish because I will never master the language, though I work at it, and work at it.

Toward the end of their lives, H. Leivick and Yankev Glatshteyn wondered if they would have any heirs. They feared that Yiddish poetry had reached the end of the line. I sense myself as their heir, more or less (*mer oder veyniker*)—an heir without their command of Yiddish, without their immersion in the world of Yiddish, without their audience (such as they had)—an insufficient heir, an interloper heir—but an heir nonetheless. Glatshteyn predicted that Yiddish poetry would reach the world through English. He was predicting me, for I am such a channel. I wish I were the fully competent heir, the heir who really knows the world he has acquired, and then takes it further, the way we think of James developing from Hawthorne, Yeats from Blake and Shelley, Larkin from Hardy. But that cannot be because of my late arrival, and because of the fate of Yiddish in the 20th century, and because of my lubberly foreign language skills. Yet, despite my late advent, despite the diminishment of Yiddish in the American scene, despite the European destruction, I am still that heir. And there are no Yiddish poets, like James, Yeats, and Larkin, who will pick up from where the 20th century Yiddish poets left off. (History dictated that if you wanted to be an important Yiddish poet it would have been better had you been born in Eastern Europe, preferably leaving before 1939.) Whatever powers of mind and art I might possess as unexpected heir I throw into that void. (Indeed, one reason I consider myself an heir of the Yiddish poets is that though early on estranged from their world and language, I later sought to possess them, scratching my way back to them. Slowly, laboriously, I have made my way to that fraternity.) Some of my poetry comes out of the works of Yiddish poets, out of my sense of how their work was neglected or not even known by young American readers (I one of them), out of the catastrophe visited upon their language and their culture. That achievement, negligence, and catastrophe attend me. I seize that condition of Yiddish poets and poetry, making my work out of the loss and inspiration they bring to me, and out of a need I originally had no idea they could reveal and gratify. That late submission to Yiddish unexpectedly drew out of me what I had heretofore rejected or concealed or simply hadn't seen—how the source of poetry can lie in the part of oneself that is at a loss, vulnerability itself the ground of poetry (that childhood lot again). The pull of Yiddish has been a great surprise to me. A linguistic decline and a historical disaster gave me a gift. I am such an heir that I have even "translated" poems whose "originals" I ascribed to a Yiddish poet, to whom I gave the name of a Yiddish writer mainly known for his prose, as if my poems were lost poems of his newly found Yiddish pseudepigrapha: "idioms poured from old brown bottles."

Now that Yiddish culture is nearing its end, the language drifts into the recesses of ourselves to become the necessary book of our lives, that book that can only emerge from affection and vulnerability, and that has a dark side and a gleaming side—the moon within us. To take shelter again in Richard Hugo's contention, there is an outrageous egotistical exploitation of subject matter that every poet must chance—Hell and the Garden of Eden through the voracious pride of Milton's mind; a religious decline sharpened through Emily Dickinson's senses; the fate of Ireland dramatized through the obsessions and contradictions of Yeats, inherent in the play of his title "Meditations in Time of Civil War."

Just as Yiddish poets took to Chinese poetry as if they had discovered a continent (Glatshteyn's way of putting it), so I discovered Yiddish poetry as if it were a continent (a submerged one, my personal Atlantis). Or our relationship calls forth another comparison. It's as if Yiddish were a woman I knew when I was young and who wanted me to go out with her but whom I rejected because I found her ugly, ungainly, and an embarrassment to be with. But when, in middle age, I met her again, I found her to be sweet, playful, alluring, and *she* hadn't changed a bit, but *I* had, and she was the woman I wanted most of all. It was, as it turned out, my good fortune to have rejected Yiddish when young. But it would have been my even better fortune to have embraced it. And my best fortune, in my egregious fantasy, to have been born, raised and educated in Vilna, getting out in time. But with "better" or "best" I would not have had my fertile tension with Yiddish, for my early resistance to Yiddish created a void that Yiddish itself would later fill.

Sometimes I'm asked: Why Yiddish rather than Hebrew? Yiddish rather than Hebrew because Yiddish is associated with my childhood and family, and with what my ear and mind received when young, when I couldn't fathom the element I was in. Yiddish was there inside my body as Hebrew never was, though I was compelled to study it in Hebrew school. I do miss knowing Hebrew because then I could read Genesis in the original. However, after reading Yehoash's translation of Genesis into Yiddish, I was convinced, enticed back to the intimacies of family conversations, that Yiddish was the ur-language of the book:

> *"Hot Lobm gezogt tsu Yankevn: Tsi vayl du bist mayner an*
> *eygener, zolstu mir dinen umzist? Zog mir vos iz dayn loyn."*
> (Genesis 29:15)

> "Laban said to Jacob, 'Just because you are a kinsman,
> should you serve me for nothing? Tell me, what shall
> your wages be?'"
> (The Jewish Publication Society)

(By the way, I'd translate that last sentence as "So, how much do you want?")

I have even deeper grounds for supposing that Yiddish is the original language of the Bible. Here is the first sentence of Genesis in Yehoash's Yiddish: *"In onheyb hot got bashafn dem himl un di erd."* The Yiddish seems so elemental, so natal, to my ears that I sense creation in the words and sounds. I don't know how to convey this sensation other than by saying that the Yiddish of Yehoash becomes the tissue of creation. It's as if I'm hearing first words within that very shaping of heaven and earth. Throughout Yehoash's Genesis I sense God possessing a Yiddish mouth and ear. The words about the creation seem less those of the Divine than of an artisan, like those of a Yiddish-speaking electrician or painter who would do work in our apartment house, wiring or spackling. The language feels close to the materials the worker is handling. Perhaps, to retreat from trope, all I am saying is that I associate Yiddish with origin, a world of speech pressing for strange possession of me from the start. Yehoash's translation of the Hebrew Bible thus re-creates two childhood impressions of mine: the Yiddish ingressions of my ears and the effects of Genesis on my imagination. Yiddish Genesis.

If, years after my childhood, I had not learned Yiddish, I would not have become a poet, or, to put it more precisely, would not have returned to poetry after putting it aside while submitting to the degrees of academic life. And then it turned out that some of my own poems emerged from that Yiddish material, and even my translations of Yiddish poetry seemed to be part of my own body of work. To return to Renato Poggioli's finely tuned essay, "The Added Artificer," "[The translator] is a character who, in finding an author without, finds also the author within." It's the transmutation of energy that Poggioli celebrates here, "this alchemy of the very making," as René Char puts it in his poem "Conduite" (in George Kalogeris's fine translation).

To enter Yiddish as an adult is to claim what I had rejected years ago—a crudeness and foreignness I also associated with my extended family, which conveniently enabled me to put them at a distance, or seemingly so. I did not finally enter Yiddish out of large cultural ambitions geared toward preservation, out of homage, renewal, kindred loyalties. My translating of Yiddish poetry does not stem from a desire to introduce people to Yiddish poetry, or to praise Yiddish and Yiddish culture, or to convey my love for Yiddish—but from some internal necessity, that kind of necessity Rilke thought was the source of poetry. If there was any fealty involved in my attachment to Yiddish, it was not to the past but to the person I had to become, the poet I had yet to become. And my obsession with the language down to its very lettering was crucial. And Yiddish became for me the conduit to a deepened self. In my childhood and pre-adolescence, Yiddish—emanating from family and neighborhood—went inside of me—both part of me and something strange and foreign. Yiddish was not "the Lake Country" of my childhood (as it is, I think, for some people I know—people who went to Yiddish schools and camps), but the language of intimate puzzlement I had felt early on, as if my early annoyance—what did it have to do with my life?—was a displaced or concealed way of wondering what did *I* have to do with my life. If what I mean by Yiddish is rightly understood—if I rightly understand it—then I can say, in a repetition that marks a cognizance I slowly came to, that if I had not finally possessed Yiddish with what I might awkwardly call an emotive intellect, I would not have become a poet—after several false starts when younger (all before I learned the language). If not the Lake Country, then daffodils is the Wordsworthian tie. When I was young and had Yiddish all about me, and in my ignorance, discomfort, and harassed attachment found it crowding in on me, I heard and heard, and connected bodies of relatives to that body of speech, "but little thought/ What wealth the show to me had brought."

Though drenched in Jewish*ness*, again like a pickle in brine, I do not translate Yiddish poetry as a way of immersing myself in some ethnic solution. I just hear the insistence of the poem: "Translate me." Tribal ties *inhere* in the language. Sociability of various kinds may follow, and that can be welcome indeed, but that's neither source nor intention. There's a remarkably candid passage by Hawthorne in his Preface to *Twice-told Tales,* a passage I read a number of times as a student and later as a teacher but did not appreciate until I read it after I left teaching and returned to writing poetry. Hawthorne says that his tales (or "sketches" as he calls them) "are not the talk of a secluded man with his own mind and heart, (had it been so, they could have hardly failed to be more deeply and permanently valuable), but his attempts, and very imperfectly successful ones, to open an intercourse with the world." Hawthorne's distinction here makes me think of what drove me to translate Yiddish poetry. It's not simply that I write about what I know (a notion that makes me squirm a bit) but that I translate from a language that has helped give me what I know. And one of the things I know is that Yiddish is the last Jewish-Diaspora language of Jewish history (there have been a number of them, but there is no need for one any more), and that finality attracts me.

A question that haunts me about my relationship to Yiddish and Yiddish poetry is: does an inveterate connection to a source of one's poetry come to narrow rather than intensify one's work? How to deepen the source and not merely rely on it? I think of how Yeats wrote his greatest poem that uses Irish mythology, "Cuchulain Comforted," at the end of his life. He finally reached that stage where his life-long attachment to that material came to a mirific culmination. And that was because through the condition of his life and his dedication to his work he had learned the magic of triumphing over his sources, that Shakespearian magic. It's not that Yeats had not achieved such triumphs earlier, but that aging had put him into an intenser relationship with some of those old materials.

I would like to stretch my condition and ally myself with the end of Yeats's "Meditations in Time of Civil War," the last section written in his favorite eight- (or elsewhere nine-) lined, rhymed stanzas, circuits of thought and confrontation with the world and himself. He leaves behind, if only temporarily, the Irish wars:

> I turn away and shut the door, and on the stair
> Wonder how many times I could have proved my worth
> In something that all others understand and share;
> But O! ambitious heart, had such a proof drawn forth
> A company of friends, a conscience set at ease,
> It had but made us pine the more. The abstract joy,

The half-read wisdom of daemonic images,
Suffice the ageing man as once the growing boy.

("Suffice" in the sense of "supply" or "replenish" or "satisfy the appetite.") Those "daemonic images" differ from poet to poet.

And then as luck would have it, I found Yeats and Yiddish making a surprising alliance, a translation of "The Second Coming" that I discovered in a Yiddish newspaper, and that took me and Yeats and Yiddish still further:

Yeats into Yiddish

der tsenter ken nit haltn . . .

Skimming the *Forverts,* I brake
for these italics—Yeats's vexation and vision
twitch in the Yiddish letters, which,
in my chronic struggle to grasp them, seem
restless, never thoroughly yielding
meaning but subsisting
in their own flourish, in
their own tremor. That quiver
of agitation in the Yiddish lettering
brings me closer to Yeats's mantic specters,
at the same time that fitful refusal
of the Yiddish letters to stay in place
predicates their power
to shift Yeats's scene from Irish wars and
Europe's carnage-births, and to conjure
pogromized Jews of the Ukraine.

I suspect (though I could be wrong) that I am the only person in the world who reads Yiddish poetry with an eye on how it will help him to write poetry in English. It is not that Yiddish rhythms inherently bear on English, but that Yiddish has become fundamental to the way I see myself, to my sense of myself in connection with the language and what it stirs in me. I am not an expert on Yiddish poetry, just a reader and a sometime translator of it. I am in love with Yiddish poetry because I am attached to the language, and not only that, but to the letters of the language, and not only that, but to the shape of the letters, and not only that, but to their sounds that enable me to imagine I might reach that goal, which, as Bruno Schulz puts it, "is to 'mature' into childhood."

Yankev Glatshteyn Visits Me in the Coffee Shop

I was facing the back
and didn't see him come in.
He shimmied into the booth
and I knew him right away.
He looked at me, clamped his lips. Sighed.
"I deliberately speak to you
in English because I want you
to understand me perfectly.
Since I died, by the way,
my English is better. I have
long conversations with Marianne Moore
about prose in poetry
and I exchange tales with Yeats—
he's not the snob he used to be.
He tells me a Celtic tale and I
tell him one about Chelm.
It's more literary the life there, but
we don't write anymore.
But that's not what I want to talk about.
It's all good and well you translate me.
You need it more than I do.
I'm in Yiddish for all time.
Not that I mind, mind you.
Be my guest. But you,
you have to translate yourself
into English. Stop fretting
about starting late. Be like Yiddish

literature—grow into your gift.
Don't brood over your unmetrical ear.
Listening to the truth-rattles in you,
your ear will catch on. By the way,
I never mourn Yiddish anymore.
We gather in Peretz's salon-cloud—
our Yiddish will last forever there—
though no one blows in from a shtetl,
manuscript in hand.
Well, *zay gezunt.*"
Absent-mindedly, he eased away the sugar-pourer,
from where it braced the laminated menu,
and his fingers played in the glass fluting;
as he moved out
he jarred the table
and my coffee shook.

2008

III

Babel

No one who takes pleasure in the variety of humanity can really be sorry that people journeyed east and began to build a tower to reach the heavens. How richer the world became after violation. Imagine, to live in a world without _____. Fill in the blank with a second language you have come to learn and love.

Must the charming and sometimes overwhelming variety of human cultures and languages only have come about through the violation committed by those builders harassed by God in the midst of their effort? We are but eleven chapters into Genesis and we have at least three major violations committed by human beings: Eating of the forbidden fruit; murder; building the tower. More than three—the evil preceding the flood. Yet it already appears that some of the violations (shall we call them "sins"?) can be productive as well as packed with sorrow, and others, like the murder of Abel, have no productive effect. How can we know which violation will really expand human possibility (even if it also carries with it grief) and which violation is only destructive? So early in the book and we are already set this difficult problem.

In this story the sin of constructing the tower leads to a variety of human languages and increase of vocabulary and the occupation of much of the world by human beings. The powers that reside in different languages themselves speak of the plenitude of humanity. (True, the story doesn't exactly say God will now create many languages, but so it has come to mean. Our interpretation of God becomes God.) Human sin has shocked God into extending the colorfulness of his original creation. After God's spreading of people around the world, there are now many ways of not only communicating among human beings but also of meditating and commenting on God. (It would almost seem that from the start of Genesis: the more we rebel against God the more He introduces variety and complexities into His original model; the more, even, He comes to face Himself, between His anger and His compassion.) Did

He diminish or expand His own conception by scattering human beings in their many languages over the face of the earth? Did He fracture His image or synthesize it through such multiple ways of talking about Him?

In its linguistic wholeness the world is sort of unified, but it becomes even more interesting (even if more dangerous) when that wholeness is broken up through human violations of divine notions. It's as if the forbidden desires of humanity force God to make the world a more interesting place than it was in the first instance. We lost Paradise, we lost our unifying language, and the world is more intriguing (and more problematical) than ever. It's the first tale about the Balkanization of the human race. Our differences—our splendor, and our dangers.

As I have said, the eleventh chapter of Genesis and we're already into Expulsion, Murder, Discord. If our glory and our horrors are intertwined, then this mixture has implications for God as well as for human beings.

Why is God so nervous about man competing with Him, yet, it almost seems, inviting him to do so? Thou shalt not eat this fruit; thou shalt not build a tower to the heavens. God takes delight in man and also fears him, distrusts him, yet dares him to match His powers—to partake of His powers and of His name, as in the story of Jacob. Oh, God, who are You that You provoke mankind? God, rejoice in Your youth.

After the abandonment of the tower and its city the world has become a place where we are forced to translate if we are to understand what is going on—and every translation is interpretation. Since the world is no longer of one speech we work for an understanding of one another. Our unity, quickly lost in Genesis, is no longer our birthright. Our understanding of one another is something we labor for. We fall in with God only to fall out again. We have to translate ourselves into ourselves.

In an economy of words the Babel story relates the prodigality of language. This is one of the paradoxes that makes Genesis the treasury of storytelling that it is. Nine verses, to tell us about the proliferation of language and vocabulary! The style itself participates in the motif; a third of the verses begin: "And they said," or "And the Lord said." Verbal economy evolves into verbal proliferation. The authors of Genesis loved their little jokes. All scholars point out the play of sounds in the story and its sarcastic punning.

This little jewel of a story, with all the brilliance of its economy, reminds us that in our proliferation of language and in our scattering on the earth God has, willy-nilly, given us a more varied world than we had before the violation. Our violation has forced Him into a re-creation even more dazzling than His first effort. As is so often the case in Genesis, the mind that plays with language is the mind that enters the uncertainty and puzzlement and change that God Himself undergoes as He watches His creation, is upset, and re-participates in it.

1993

Sarah's Laugh

"Why did Sarah laugh?" (Genesis 18:13). Some answers immediately come to mind, one even stated by Sarah, "Shall I indeed bear a child when I am old?" She may also laugh because she thinks that if this news of her childbearing turns out to be true, she spoke too hastily years before when she advised Abraham to have a child through Hagar. In that case, her laugh mocks her earlier advice.

But who are these men that bring her such unexpected and evocative news? Maybe it would be best if she claimed she never laughed. But then she is caught in the rhythms of an old game: "I didn't laugh." "Oh yes you did." "Oh no I didn't." "Yes you did. We all heard you." Her old resentments at being overlooked make her look silly and exposed right now.

And what *kind* of laugh was it? We are told that she laughed to herself, but the Lord, or those angel-guests, heard her. Was it simply a private laugh of incredulity? Or a catch in the throat from the hurt of having been denied all those years? Or did it also contain some grunt of preposterousness, or senescent lewdness, or relief at returning to Abraham's sexual keep after that visit to Egypt? Abraham's initial reaction to the news, when he leans of it earlier, is that of nervous laughter.

Kafka (the greatest secular writer of Midrash) tells several parables about Abraham, an Abraham who, he imagines, "would have never gotten to be a patriarch or even an old-clothes dealer." One of those parables of Kafka I want to relate to Sarah: This is about an Abraham who could not bring himself to sacrifice his son because though he wants to act according to his faith, he cannot believe that God would choose an unworthy person like himself to do such a deed. Perhaps there was some mistake in God calling on him and thus he is afraid that the world will laugh at him. Abraham fears he might come unsummoned. It is as if at the end of the year, when the best student was solemnly about to receive a prize, the worst student rose in the expectant stillness and came forward from his dirty desk in the last row because he had made a mistake of hearing, and the whole class burst out laughing. And perhaps he had made no mistake at all, his name really was called, it having been the teacher's intentions to make the rewarding of the best student at the same time a punishment for the worst one.

Sarah laughs because she was embarrassed in the face of a miracle. She has the fear of it all being a mistake, somehow not worthy of her: "The miracle of giving birth at an absurdly old age?" "Me, who hasn't had a period in forty years?" "Me, whom God has overlooked?" "My drooping breasts will give suck to a child?"

Behind her embarrassment, her disbelief, may also lie the thought that if God and His angels came at this late date to tell her that she will soon be with child, why couldn't He or they have arrived decades earlier with such news? Why did they wait so long? Is not that proof that she is unworthy of this conception? How come, all of a sudden, can she become worthy of this birth now? Is it possible that out of her old body will come a new body? What is this that is being visited upon her? Who are these guests, a bunch of comedians?

She cannot, does not, know how to receive this news from God. Sarah turns aside when, to borrow a phrase from the Yiddish poet, Kadya Molodovsky, she becomes "a brief guest at wonder" ("*a kirtser gast baym vunder*").

Sarah cannot bring herself to this wonder that God, belatedly, is bringing to her. She only feels her embarrassment in the face of the divine force, just what Abraham feels in Kafka's version of the biblical story.

Sarah's laugh is the opening laughter in the tradition of Jewish skepticism or sarcasm about sacred stratagems, leading eventually to the redoubtable genre of the Jewish joke. (That the joke in this case turns out to be on the laughing skeptic only shows how deep the joke runs.) And the joke takes an odd twist when just before Sarah does conceive she is associated with both fertility and barrenness: "and God healed Abimelech, his wife, and his slave-girls, and they bore children; for the Lord had made every woman in Abimelech's household barren on account of Abraham's wife Sarah" (20:17-18).

Again, and almost in conclusion, what is her laugh like: A saucy, "That'll be the day"? A challenging, "Who are you kidding?" A scoffing, "I'll believe it when I see it"? A prideful, "It's about time"? Or could it even be a laughter of secret relief, "At last God looks at me, chooses me, favors my womb"? Or is it the laughter that comes off of bad timing, "Now he promises me"? Or, maybe, winking at Abraham, she throws up to the angels a Yiddish proverb about their Sender, "If God wills it, even a broom can shoot." (*Az got vil, shist a bezem oykh.*)

Yet the matter of her laughter does not quite end there, for after giving birth to Isaac she says, "God has given me good reason to laugh and everybody will laugh with me" (21:6). She has a new take on her own skeptical laughter as new life does indeed come out of her old body. She becomes the literal channel of the remarkable birth; she has both the first and the last laugh. We share her laughter—struck as we are by the barren, ill-used and resentful wife who at last becomes fertile.

Our matriarch.

1995

In Moriah

They don't speak, they are unnamed, and we are told nothing about them—the two servants who accompany Abraham and Isaac to the land of Moriah. They aren't needed for saddling the ass, since Abraham does that. They don't cut the wood for the burnt offering, since Abraham does that too. And he himself loads the wood on his son's back, just as earlier he himself set Ishmael on the shoulder of Hagar along with bread and water. (You can, like Abraham with his sons, be hard in following God; and you can, like Jonah, be hard in disobeying God.)

The servants travel with Abraham and Isaac for three days as they "set out for the place of which God has spoken." Did they notice nothing? Suspect nothing? Was Abraham the perfect dissembler—in appearance, in speech, in the preparations for ritual?

"When we have worshipped we will come back to you," says Abraham to the servants. Perhaps they merely serve as a conversational cover for Abraham's true intentions. Did they never wonder where the animal was to be sacrificed? Did they hear no unusual tone in Abraham's "we"?

These two servants exist in the shadow of the great man and his son, in the shadow of God's intentions and promise. They are removed from the great event and probably not affected by the ensuing promises to Abraham's descendants. On his return from the sacrifice, was there nothing in Abraham's countenance—no sign of relief, or amazement—they could have picked up? Nothing in the demeanor of Isaac? No pallor? No falter? No glaze?

It is not the fate of these two servants to hear the word of the angel of the Lord. Yet they have the power to wonder or not wonder about what is going on, assuming something unusual comes through to them. But perhaps nothing like that is conveyed, and this is just a six-day assignment on the road—three days out, three days back. And back home, when asked, "How did it go?" they simply answer "O.K." Of do they suspect something but refuse to speculate? How

95

can they know?

What did they do when Abraham and Isaac were away? Play cards, take a snooze, gossip, toss stones, feed the ass, tell stories? (To tell a story while an even greater one is occurring in which you play a minor part!)

Did they wonder why Abraham and Isaac had to travel so far in order to make the sacrifice, and then even further, without them, to reach the exact spot? Why was the sacrifice done out of their sight? Was that something to wonder about, or just the way masters sacrifice, leaving their servants out of eyeshot and earshot?

Did they pick up no snatches of odd conversation between Abraham and Isaac on their return? Did they notice any marks left on Isaac since he had been bound and his back was laid out directly on the wood? No pieces of bark sticking to his skin, or hair, or clothing? Nothing, nothing at all?

Was there absolutely nothing different about Abraham and Isaac on their return? Or did they notice something and choose not to talk about it? What if one saw and one didn't, and the former was persuaded by the latter? Perhaps only a suspicious mind, and one inviting trouble, would think of connecting this trip to Abraham's sending Ishmael away.

Nameless, apparently with nothing even to wonder about, these servants seem not to be in history, not even as bystander. Myth has passed them by. They stand outside a vision, a powerful psychological moment, a defining event. Is it really possible that all is hidden from them? Or do they help all to be hidden from them? Do they suspect nothing? Do they even say within themselves: "We'll never know." "Who can tell?" "Who knows?" "Nah, couldn't be"?

Did they ever come to know that Abraham named the place of sacrifice "Adonai yireh": that mount "where the Lord is seen" or, on the mount "of the Lord there is vision" or "there is sight"? Did they know that at all? If so, was it to them just the name of a place? A place has to be named something, like "First Encounter Beach" or "Salem." Was there absolutely nothing for them to construe, guess at, try out on their tongue, or even entertain with a closed mouth "hmmm"?

Are these two servants representatives of some impaired condition shorn of all powers of speculation—bare, naked, infertile—without power or authority or curiosity—without urge to contemplate, wonder, entertain?

They are not silent witnesses of evil (whom we have heard so much about in our time), but those who lack the inclination, the spur, the luck, the motivation, the condition, to reflect at all on a divine moment or revelation, the moment God enters human experience, shapes destiny. These servants do not have a clue. Or is it that they won't see one? Or aren't permitted one?

These servants seem to be in the story only to be written out of it. They are there to serve but not to know. Is there some way they could have been made to see they were part of a momentous event—a story engaged with God, with a father and son, with terror, reprieve and promise? Is there some way to include them in the depths of the story, or do *they* take themselves out of it? They service the divine moment but are not included in it. Are they too low for vision, or, like Balaam at first, too high? Their silence intimates some part of ourselves. Ignored before, they now stand out. We are drawn by the strange appeal of matter that refuses to fall into place, that will not fit (especially when once that's all it did!).

And yet, finally, perhaps the role of these servants is simple— to stay with the ass, to make sure the beast of burden is not stolen. The material accessories but not the participants in the vision, they wait.

1997

Jacob's Struggle

A good piece of writing has the knack of surviving itself, including its very power to turn into a cliché, as the image of the wrestling Jacob has become a cliché of religious and personal struggle.

One usual interpretation of the scene is that through the encounter Jacob becomes Israel; that is, he turns from the old conniving self into Patriarch, the groundwork for which is laid in the earlier scene in which he dreams of the angels moving between two realms. Jacob has a dream going out and a spiritual encounter coming back. The conniver and thief turn into a spiritual hero, a Jewish Hermes. Without a role in the divine narrative, Jacob, with all his native skills, might have ended up selling junk bonds.

Despite his change, Jacob still shows signs of the old self. In the rest of the narrative he is sometimes called Jacob, sometimes Israel. We find Cunning Jacob, Obsequious Jacob, Promethean Jacob, Transformed Jacob. How does one change? Who would trust one's "new self" if it bore no relationship to the "old one," if it didn't sometimes relapse or show old features? No reliability without recidivism.

Yet, we might imagine, how tired Jacob must be of his own history of contrivances, disguises, counter-ploys—all those skills of manipulation. Something is getting ready to fall away, or nearly fall away, or occasionally fall away.

Even after the wrestling match, he has not so changed as to make an outright apology to his brother, whose graciousness is evident—"Let us set out and I will go at your pace," which may refer not only to Jacob's retinue but also to his limp. Still, when Esau asks, in what almost feels like an antiquated language of the street, "What was all that company of yours I met?" Jacob responds, at last with candor, "It was meant to win favor with you, my lord." "My lord" is repeated four more times, Jacob, the old smoothie, at work again (and he does have reason to fear his brother, we must admit).

Change isn't easy, even after you've been toe-to-toe with God or one of His designated wrestlers. Still and all, Jacob is being transformed, to the point further on when, presumably, he can grasp the origins of the deception of his own sons in their reaction to the rape of Dina. One of the reasons Jacob does not criticize his sons more severely than he does is that he knows his own past is implicated in their behavior. There is a midrash that shortly before his sons commit their perfidious act, Jacob discovers among his belongings the goat skins he wore when he deceived his father. But Jacob *also* knows, as his sons do not, that a person (like Shechem) can commit a dishonorable act, regret it, and change. (I can't think of any other tale in which rape turns into love, though there are many in which love turns into rape, as with Amnon and Tamar in Second Samuel.)

The theme of the son who deceives the father and who in turn is deceived by his own sons is not only a psychological pivot in Genesis but one of the many indications that God deals in all kinds of "merchandise" to advance His sacred narrative. Sometimes it seems He has the morality of an artist.

Why is the encounter between Jacob and the divine figure a combined maiming and blessing?

A secular or psychological interpretation of this hands-on encounter is evoked in a famous passage of Keats (a passage that grows on one), who called the world "The Vale of Soul-Making" and in a letter to his brother and sister-in-law explained,

> Do you not see how necessary a World of Pains and troubles is
> to school an Intelligence and make it a soul? A Place where the
> heart must feel and suffer in a thousand diverse ways.
> (April 21, 1815)

Jacob is on his way from being an intelligence to becoming a soul. He struggles with that divine figure precisely at the point he has "crossed over" not only to become a new person but to examine who he has been all along. Camus could have written an entire essay just on that moment between the time "Jacob was left alone" and that figure appeared.

A mythical interpretation of the encounter lies in the suggestion that Jacob's wrestling with God (or one of His agents) is a Promethean-like experience. God is both source and opponent. Indeed, our very opposition brings us closer to Him. We sometimes feel most vivified by feeling we have stolen some god-like power for ourselves. In this religious/mythical interpretation, we are rivals of God in His creation. He created us to be so. And God (or the gods) as well as we may be ambivalent about the relationship. It appears from this story that the divine figure could have won the battle, having severely wounded Jacob, but declines to do so, as if the divine force welcomes the struggle with the opponent, Jacob, the human being, yet still must leave a painful reminder in the body of the human contestant. Jacob isn't wounded in the socket of the shoulder or in the elbow or in the wrist because the wound has to do with where he has come from and where he is going.

It's one of the great ironies of the spirit (often observed) that unless we make life out of life we are doomed to a spiritual death. And the most challenging task of such an effort is to take our energy from what we consider the source of those energies—God, nature, the unconscious. Touching that source, even matching ourselves against it, revivifies us, but the energy that creates is also the energy that wounds, or does not easily yield itself up, or without a price— hence Jacob's limp, cousin, you might say, to the pegleg stalk of Captain Ahab.

In Gauguin's painting "Jacob Wrestling with the Angel," an angel with golden wings holds Jacob in what looks like a hammer lock; Jacob's neck is wrenched downward. But what is really noteworthy about the painting is that the biblical scene is "shot" from over the heads of onlooking Breton peasant women and their priest, who are enthralled. The women are looking at the scene they were told about in church that morning. A tree that seems to turn into a river slashes across the canvas. The women, some on their knees, praying, look across it as they take in the scene. Their concentration, their prominent, lappet-like bonnets that turn into white emblems of astonishment, the way that river-tree cuts into some of them—all this suggests that what they are undergoing is not a Sabbath lesson but an event in their lives.

1998

Jacob's Head

Here, I am with you,
I will watch over you wherever you go
and will bring you back to this soil;
indeed, I will not leave you
until I have done what I have spoken to you.
Jacob awoke from his sleep
and said:
Why,
the Lord is in this place,
and I, I did not know it!
(Genesis 28:15-16)*

Deceit and flight have led to vision, discovery, and dedication, eventually to Jacob's changed manhood. His dream, occurring just before this passage, comes to him while his head rests on a stone. The hard pillow is turned into a sacred pillar. (Word play often comes easier than the hard experience it points to.)

Jacob discovers God in the least place we would expect to find Him—in his exile, in his going from home to a new place. What began as a son dutifully following his mother's scheme for advancement, as a trick played on his brother, as double dealing, turns into dream and the fulfilling of God's purpose.

Nahum Sarna points out that neither Abraham nor Isaac exhibits surprise at his initial experience of God's sudden revelation, but Jacob does. He is startled. Sarna posits that Jacob is shaken because of his sense of unworthiness. He doesn't expect that God would appear to someone like him.

Jacob's connection to God is sudden, unexpected and dramatic (the dream of the divine figures ascending and descending). Yet it is also calculated when he awakes: if he can get back safely to his

---

* The passage is from Everett Fox's translation *The Five Books of Moses*, except that I have substituted Jacob for Yaakov and the Lord for YHWH.

father's house he will make the Lord his God.

Jacob—the man who has had the greatest vision of his life, yet who still haggles with God. The man who has visions is not necessarily the man of faith, not even of absolute faith in his visions.

Jacob is the man who answers *yes* to a vexing question Whitman puts in *Song of Myself*. Whitman, or the absorbent narrator of the poem, is visited by God, "a loving bedfellow," who has slept by his side all night and has left behind "baskets covered with white towels bulging the house with their plenty." After this fecund visitation, Whitman asks,

> Shall I postpone my acceptation and realization and scream
>   at my eyes,
> That they turn from gazing after and down the road,
> And forthwith cipher and show me to a cent,
> Exactly the contents of one, and exactly the contents of two,
>   and which is ahead?
>
>   (Section 3)

(There is a prophet-like clamor in Whitman's phrasings.)

Jacob both receives the vision and postpones his full "acceptation" by attaching a proviso to it—Jacob's codicil of calculation.

Jacob is both calculator and visionary. The maneuvering gets him through his relationships, often necessarily so. The visions connect him to God but also to other people, and to a side of himself he was previously not aware of. Despite himself, he is carried from a hard place (that stone-pillow) to a sense of deeper devotion in his life. Legend has it that Jacob had a number of dreams during his trek from Beersheba to Harran, perhaps signs that he is trying to imagine a new life for himself out of old, hard material, like that stone on which his head lies.

In some ways, Jacob is of poor material. Our material. Then he is shocked to find out what can move him—and the act of deceit which changes his life is followed by dreams which further change his life.

Jacob—in flight, or exile—discovers God in a place where he would not have expected to find Him, a place where God could do His work on him. The condition of his exile, his aloneness, his sleep, his simultaneous travel outward and inward has turned into the realm of his dedication. And now Jacob struggles to be worthy of his life, or of what has been shown to him. His head has literally been *on* the hard place, and it is there where divine figures appear and God speaks. At the same time, at the same place, Jacob offers contingent commitments.

When we read of key moments in the life of a character in a story, we are only convinced by the intensity of the experience, its ineluctable specifics—in this case, stone, ladder, voice, oil. And the brother-son-man out to seek his fortune in the world is transformed—convincingly so because the transformation is sudden visitation, contingency, and lifelong task (not without payment far down the line for who he was when young). Furthermore, visions immediately followed by qualifications set up by the visionary might have a special appeal to our state of mind, i.e., to a skeptical yet yearning mind.

Though Jacob's head lying on the stone holds the dream of angels ascending and descending, the trickery of his mother and his willingness to go along lead him, it turns out, to that vision in the desert. Jacob did not know, originally, what forces were going to operate in his life. Something else is calling to him, to this runaway, to the very condition of his flight and the reason for it:

> Why,
> the Lord is in this place,
> and I, I did not know it!

Out of what was originally such petty material—scheming, rivalry, jealousy—the dreck of family relations—comes eventually the calling, the vision, the sacred place, the dedication.

Just stopping somewhere, between Beersheba and Harran, because it is getting toward night, Jacob lays his head on a stone. And he dreams in this place and then gives it a name, Beth-El, House of God. (What a source for the name of so many architecturally complacent synagogues in America!) From such hardness, where Jacob's head lay, comes the vision of divine figures going up and going down:

> Why,
> the Lord is in this place,
> and I, I did not know it!

Jacob's vision has convincing power about it precisely because he is startled by it; that is to say, startled by his own life that has had the vision, which also drives him back upon himself: *so that's who I was, so that's how I thought.* The man who still thinks the way he used to think lives alongside the man who has visions that insist he change his life. The man who connives is also the man who imagines a new life for himself. The onomastic split—sometimes Jacob, sometimes Israel—may reflect the torn self of the character.

Jacob enters, you might say grows into, his complexity, grows into it during the flight he undertakes because of his falseness. This immersion in the layered self is one way of conceiving of the soil he will be brought back to, as God tells Jacob He will not leave him until He has done what He has promised him. For that soil can be conceived of as Jacob's own homeland—that is, the homeland of vision, of contradiction, of self-scrutiny, of "soul-making." Jacob's turmoil becomes his task, and he awakes, telling himself:

> Why,
> the Lord is in this place,
> and I, I did not know it!

1999

In Horeb

It's your average workday. Moses goes with his flock into the wilderness, comes to Horeb and then sees something extraordinary: a bush on fire that is not consumed by that fire. Some say it was a sign of Moses' worthiness that he stopped to look, and indeed we are told, "When the Lord saw that he [Moses] had turned aside to look, God called to him out of the bush." But really, if we stop to think about it, only a dullard wouldn't stop to look at a burning bush that remained itself and was not destroyed by its own fire, that even, according to one midrash, bore blossoms as it was burning (a fancy of great theological import).

It's not because Moses stopped to look that God chose him, calling to him from out of the bush. What is important is that Moses saw it, had a vision, and in that vision lies his conversion to the belief in the Hebrew God. This episode has all the earmarks (and eyemarks) of a similar conversion described by William James in *The Varieties of Religious Experience:*

> How real, definite and memorable an event sudden conversion may be to him who has the experience . . . undergoer of an astounding process performed upon him from above . . . the spirit of God is with us at these dramatic moments in a peculiarly miraculous way, unlike what happens at any other juncture of our lives. At that moment . . . an absolutely new nature is breathed into us, and we become partakers of the very substance of the Deity.

I also think of the burning coal brought to the lips of Isaiah, or of Ezekiel's vision of four-faced and four-winged beings, eyes on the rims of wheels intersecting and moving, a vault-like glittering ice, and a radiant figure on a throne. (Ezekiel must have read Blake.) However, one must also understand that the act of purifying Isaiah's lips with the burning coal (powerfully summoned up in a cheder scene in *Call It Sleep,* in the child's urge to be clean, to be endowed by light) is not an end in itself, for it leads to other things, Isaiah's vigorous declaration about justice and right worship.

It's not that God chose Moses because he had the curiosity to stop and look but that Moses envisioned the burning bush and heard God speak out of that blaze. But that's not all: for from that vision which Moses undergoes—and here is the curious wrinkle of this mystical experience—Moses takes on a social task. "Come, therefore," says God to Moses, "I will send you to Pharaoh, and you shall free my people, the Israelites from Egypt."

Moses is not so much the man of faith (Abraham is the man in that regard) as he is the man who has a mystical experience by means of which God leads him to political and social leadership. God spoke to Moses from the burning bush in order to give Moses this specific task. Moses is, indeed, the first of the prophets.

The power of such visions is that even when they lead to the social ends of freedom and the making of culture by one's own group, they lend a curve beyond that concept of justice that has so gripped the Jewish mind, that lies so deep in Jewish thought. One of the appeals of Hassidism in its early years of glory, and Abraham Heschel points this out somewhere, is that it combined miracle stories with the ethical—surely, by the way, one of the reasons I. L. Peretz was so compelled to re-work those stories, compelled to bring their moral and narrative aura into the context of his own skepticism. I think that Peretz would have understood how it can be a passionate thing to talk about the God you don't believe in. As a matter of fact the very lack of belief can be a spring to the theological imagination. It would be a defeat for that imagination, and for God, if He only belonged to the religious.

The Jewish God who demands the practice of justice (even though He Himself does some wild things to his wayward people) is an impressive God (as we know from the powerful passage from Isaiah we read during Yom Kippur [57:14–58:14], or from that instruction in guilt, repentance and redemption we read in the Book of Jonah). And the two rabbis I have most admired, both Hillel directors, have had a strong sense of social justice. But I think I see an even greater God residing in that bush that burns but is not consumed, the bush that says, in the famous words of the Yiddish poet, H. Leivick, "I burn and I burn and I'm not consumed." *"Ikh bren un ikh bren un ikh ver nit farbrent,"* a line by the way, that sentimentalists quote in support of their notion of an eternity of Yiddish. (Metaphors can mislead and block us from the truth as much as they can open us up to it.) I think I see that even greater God who appears in a pillar of cloud and a pillar of fire, who rises from the night to wrestle with Jacob, who appears in the midst of the Garden of Eden and asks Adam, "Where are you?"who commands Abraham to sacrifice his son, who tries to kill Moses seemingly because he isn't circumcised, who speaks to Moses out of the burning bush. These are the presences of the Jewish God that hold me most of all, presences I remember meeting in my childhood texts of Genesis and Exodus (darkly illustrated by Doré). The Jewish God whose miracles are attached to the moral development of human beings is a magnificent God. The Jewish God whose miracles are beyond moral comprehension may be an even greater God.

It is the God of miracle (who appears during the working day) and the God of contradiction who fascinates me most of all. Not the God who gives Moses the Ten Commandments, but the God who in Isaiah says,

> I am the Lord and there is none else,
> I form light and create darkness,
> I make weal and create woe—
> I the Lord do all these things.

(45:6-7)

The paradoxical truth is that if the world made sense and we felt secure about existence we would not need God. Out of our need to shape our lives from within their very perils comes that drive to contemplate and re-contemplate God. In that re-shaping and imagining, Jews have yet to face the limitations of monotheism. Jews may be a people too anxious to make the world cohere. (Call that coherency *the Joseph principle*, since he tells his brothers not to be distressed for having sold him into slavery. It was God who had sent him to Egypt. I have even consoled myself with the Joseph principle.)

How inadequate is J. H. Hertz's note (in his edition of *The Pentateuch and Haftorahs*) quoting the rabbis in response to Exodus 3:7 about the affliction of the children of Israel in Egypt: "God always takes the side of the persecuted." If Hertz didn't exist I would have to create him, for he is a stand-in for all those rabbis since my cheder years who I found inadequate because they reeked of the notion: "See, if you only read the Bible in the right way, it all coheres, it all works out." Thus it is with great affection and need that I read Hertz, for in his notes he reminds me of who I am by what I have rejected. It is not the promise of wholeness, of eventual coherence, that is so engaging about Torah, but the act of engagement itself, which Moses initiates through his vision, not because he stopped to look but because he carried something within himself that God spoke to and shaped in all of its dedication, tensions, and contradictions.

The burning bush could be an image of God who is defined out of His very destruction into existence. (That midrash of the bush bearing blossoms in the burning!) And to comprehend God's life moving out of His death—his burning away into further existence— is what Moses really comes to see in the burning bush. God is consumed, long live God. I also think of the bushes and trees of Van Gogh that seem to burn in their very coming to shape—fiery and alive, their writhing self-consummation the very guarantee of their existence, as if every brush stroke were a flame. The great paradox in Moses' vision is that the fire that destroys can become the fire that sustains. This is the fire that Moses sees in Horeb, and his life is changed.

That burning bush—our Jewish phoenix!

1999

Zipporah's Touch

In a letter to his fiancée, Kafka talks of our letting "the dark complexity of Judaism, which contains so many unpenetrable features, do its work." Kafka is an appropriate guide to such complexities because his stories, in the words of Gershom Scholem, "walk a fine line between religion and nihilism."

In Chapter 4 of Exodus, verses 24-26, we read about Moses:

> At a night encampment on the way, the Lord encountered him and sought to kill him. So Zipporah took a flint and cut off her son's foreskin, and touched his legs with it, saying, "You are truly a bridegroom of blood to me!" And when He let him alone, she added, "A bridegroom of blood because of the circumcision."

Zipporah, Moses' wife, cuts off her son's foreskin. By being smeared with his son's blood, Moses is circumcised symbolically. But the passage is not clear because in part the pronoun references are not clear, as all commentators have noted. It's even argued that the passage is an interpolation because it interrupts the narrative, though it actually strengthens the narrative as well as the character of Moses and follows the sentence just before it, where God tells Moses to tell Pharoah that He will slay his firstborn son if he doesn't relent and allow the kinsmen of Moses to worship Him. From that warning we go to the wounding of Moses' son, as if God wants Moses to face, in this anticipatory, safe way, the shedding of blood that is inherent in the struggle whose leader he is on the way to becoming. (How bloody the necessary acts of liberation, the lives it costs!—We see that over and over.) After gazing at the burning bush that doesn't burn up and hearing a voice calling to him from out of that bush and after this scene of circumcision and right of passage, Moses must sense the intertwining of terror and identity.

It is as if through this episode God tells Moses: "Absorb irrationality and terror into your vision of a new identity and freedom. And you will face irrationalities within Me Myself."

This is of course not the first time in Torah that we have seen the presence of the demonic in the divine, as when, in that primal struggle for identity and continuation, Jacob wrestles with an angel, or God. Or, we read later on, that death can be visited upon someone who comes too close to the divine—"Any man who touches the mountain [Sinai] must be put to death" (Exodus 19:21). An ominous feature of the divine is displayed in II Samuel (6:6-7): "when they came to a certain threshing-floor, the oxen [pulling the cart that carries the ark] stumbled, and Uzzah reached out to the Ark of God and took hold of it. The Lord was angry with Uzzah and struck him down there for his rash act. So he died there beside the Ark of God." David is vexed by the scene, and asks himself, "How can I harbor the Ark of the Lord after this?" And, indeed, many a Jew has never again touched the Ark or Torah after witnessing or hearing about God's irrationalities or His inexplicable behavior, even though God at one point covers himself in this passage I can't shake off:

I am the Lord and there is none else,
I form light and create darkness,
I make weal and create woe—
I the Lord do all these things.

(Isaiah 45:6-7)

These are among the most disturbing yet also stimulating words God utters in the Bible. Abraham Heschel speaks of the need to "imbue the Jew with the courage to fear God." The word "courage" there is as important as the word "fear." I use Heschel's phrase short of the assuredness he must have ultimately meant.

What a path Moses takes: the killing of the Egyptian and hiding him in the sand, the bush that burns but is not destroyed, the bloody smear after the vicarious circumcision—a few of the conditions through which Moses comes into his true task: leader, channel of plagues, angry bearer of laws, as well as pleader, consoler, explainer, mother-figure—that complex role he finally submits to—

his entanglement in the living God, that mixture of frightfulness and life we sense in that incident of symbolic circumcision!

We discover in Exodus 18:2 that Moses later on dismisses his wife, and she and her two sons are received by her father, Jethro. Moses, as we often find with heroes, separates from his family as he more and more takes on the heroic task. If we think of Zipporah as psychological force rather than an actual person, she can now retire from the scene, having served her function. Moses is ready to meet the destructive powers, even utilize them, and move through them to his goals. There is a profound pause in the passage I'm focusing on here. After Zipporah touches Moses' leg with the foreskin and says to him, "You are truly a bridegroom of blood to me!" we reach that pause, "And when He let him alone. . . ." Then she adds, "A bridegroom of blood because of the circumcision." That is, she sees that the act of touching Moses with the bloody foreskin works; it keeps him safe, and he is now married to the force of life beyond the threatening demon. She has played her role in freeing him to play his. (So far as I know, Zipporah is the only woman in all of literature who circumcises her own son and then, symbolically, her husband. This is *not* a case of symbolic castration, for in her removal of part of the male sexual organ she protects her son and husband from the destructive powers.)

It was quick-witted Zipporah who enabled Moses to go on with his public-religious tasks. Zipporah, in this incident, possesses a force that enables Moses to get past the demon. She is the one who starts the blood, saving her son and husband thereby—a Medea-figure who is life-giving.

Once, in Israel, I saw the slaughtering of sheep by Samaritans in preparation for the Seder. After killing the sheep they smeared the blood of the sheep on their sons who, presumably, were thereby saved from destructive forces and made part of the community, their faces becoming substitutes for the blood-smeared doorposts and lintels in the Exodus story (12:22).

Moses has escaped some dreadful experience through the

shrewdness of his mother/wife who instinctively understands that, to be saved from the demands of the demon, Moses must be touched by blood from the foreskin itself, that head of potency, if you will. He must be touched *in a protective way* by the blood, the flesh, the demon wants *all of.* Meeting the demonic *partly* on its own terms is a way of preserving Moses for the great tasks he is to undertake. To come back to the destructive element and thereby to be empowered for the great tasks seems to be at stake here. We also see in other passages from the Bible that the demonic and the holy are interconnected, and the character who is so engaged is marked for life. This piece of flesh that is cut off and that touches Moses enables him to ward off a destructive force *even as he is touched by it*—this is the wit, the understanding, of Zipporah in this passage, as Moses is then freed to go on to face his fear of incompetency, the hard facts of political evil, his own use of power, the long dangerous trek to identity, his later encounters with God—that demon, that divinity.

1999

God Sews

How many times I have read Genesis, and how many times found scenes, or sentences, or phrases, or words I'd never noticed before, or noticed and forgot. So I feel about the sentence of Genesis 3:21—"And the Lord God made garments of skins for Adam and his wife, and clothed them." It's as if someone had inserted that sentence between the last time I read Genesis and this time.

When I read these lines I don't think of God saying "Presto"— as when he says, "Let there be light"—and suddenly Adam and Eve are clothed, a magical investiture, like in a movie. No, here is no cosmographic abracadabra. In fact, no locution or conjuration at all. Rather, I see Him, the first *shnayder* (Yiddish for tailor), sitting down and stitching the garments, handing them to Adam and Eve, and eyeing them to make sure the skins fit.

Here's Yehoash's translation of the sentence from his superb Yiddish translation of the Bible: "*Un got der har hot gemakht far odemen un zayn vayb hemdlekh fun fel, un hot zey bakleydt.*" My fancy is that the reader or speaker of Yiddish can hear in Yehoash's sentence a description of the first Jewish tailor at work. The Yiddish reader might hear something of the needle trades in *gemakht* ("made"), *hemdlekh* ("shirts"), *bakleydt* ("clothed"). God—founding member of the first shirtwaist makers' union, or the furriers' union (though He may have found the latter too leftist for his taste).

I think of this act of sewing as God's first stitch of work, as distinct from the magic creation of the first six days, as distinct from the breath-magic of the creation of Adam, as distinct from the sleight-of-hand surgery that drew forth Eve, as distinct from the evocation of animal, seed and fruit—yet which lead into this fine work of fixing. I see Him in His stitching partaking of the kind of labor He now assigns to Adam and Eve, thereby showing them how He is invested in their fate, attached to their work. (He might almost be singing a Shaker hymn as he pieces together the pelts.) Sewing them their first garment is His acknowledgement not only that He owes them something, but that in creating them He has learned something about His responsibilities, as He too is obliged to make some effort to provide for them even in their transgression. One of the reasons Genesis is my favorite book of the Bible is that God is so intimately involved with the fate of its characters. He lives down the hall, you might say.

It's as if in making their garments, God says to Adam and Eve, "See, even in your exile, I am with you; you wear what I have made, and you have prompted me to add to my original creation. In my cursing you and banishing you, you compel me to continue my creation. I see now I have something further to do. You have brought me to your level. I clothe you, now go." God and the human beings He has created make a bargain.

Here is God, after six days of large scale creation, turning to sewing skins for the first two human beings, God changed to the maker of elemental clothing. I see God humbled by His own creation into a deeper sense of Himself, moved by what He has learned about human beings, bent over the skins at the exact task of cutting and sewing. God, *der shnayder.*

God is forced to move beyond His own intention in creating the world and human beings, past His own pre-conceptions, to become aware of the implications of what He has done. The idea of God discovering Himself, and changing, is one of the great ideas of the Jewish God. Thinking about God the tailor leads me to work up a phrase from Carlyle's *Sartor Resartus (The Tailor Retailored—Der Shnayderibergeshnaydert* in my forthcoming Yiddish translation)— leads me, as I was saying, to the phrase "a clothes theology."

How impoverished we would be if God Himself did not find instruction in what He originally put together. God made better than what He intended through the impairment and mending of His initial fit. (Part of what I mean by "clothes theology.") His own errors or lack of foresight (or mismeasurement, to inch the metaphor along) keeps Him aware, gives Him possibilities of perceiving beyond His initial design. Without His miscalculations, there'd be no living

God, who ended up "clothing Adam and Eve for a world," which as Milton's angel Michael tells Adam, with the right faith and deeds will become an even happier world than the one they left behind. God, in both the Bible and *Paradise Lost*, has gone from His perfect measurements to risk and possibility. Go, Milton's angel tells Adam, go and tell the news to Eve.

Even if we assume that God exists because we create the God that we need, something happens in the process—that the God we create comes to create us in turn. There's a reciprocal birthing here.

I imagine God thinking beyond what we read in Genesis 3:21: "I began with bursts of creation. Coming out of that, I now sit and sew." God is humbled, brought down from Universe Maker to tailor. He discovers He has designed a mistake—or, an imperfection—and in being brought down to our level, His Plan gone awry, He must learn how to make Himself again. God was defeated—beaten back— by His own creation, but to equip the creatures that failed Him He came and sewed them garments, adding skin to skin. God comes to learn that what He thought He wanted was itself a mistake, and that leads Him to new ways of conceiving of Himself. (The reassessing voices of God, torn over His handiwork, must have startled the prophets into writing.)

Thus the God I imagine. For what I am after is a skeptic's theology; that is—to play off a well-known remark by Wallace Stevens, that atheist-religious poet—God is a fiction that our intelligence and imagination needs. Why that is so is something of a mystery to me, but I sense all kinds of powers in that fabrication.

2000

The Chance to Dream

By and large, biblical dreams are not Freudian dreams (the night-poem of the personal), though there are exceptions, as when Joseph dreams that he will have dominion over his brothers and his father. Biblical dreams usually do not come from the psyche of the dreamer (and even when they do they are theo-psychic). Through dreams, God shows us that He commands the dreamer and the life beyond the dreamer.

What is most important about dreams in the Bible is that the dreamer is compelled to live (or die) by the dream. The point of the dream is not that it needs to be interpreted (though that is usually necessary and such interpretive talents can lead to a career, as in the cases of Joseph and Daniel*) but that it needs to be followed—that the dreamer must put his life at the behest of the power of the dream. In the Bible, dream is fate.

In the Bible, dreams come from God and drive the life of the dreamer. We witness a theological history, a God-driven panorama of events in which the Pharoah's dreams are related to Joseph's earlier dreams, for through Joseph's interpretations of the Pharoah's dreams his own earlier ones are realized, leading finally to the long Jewish march to its own being.

It's not, as I say, that dreams in the Bible can't be revelatory of the dreamer, as Solomon's dream (I Kings 3:4-15) is your basic dream as wish—"Now, what do I want most of all?" But of course that dream is related to Solomon's stewardship and God's plans of

---

*Daniel is the most intriguing dream interpreter in the Bible. He is not only granted those powers by God but also possesses a highly sophisticated education. He can not only interpret dreams that are beyond the understanding of Chaldean magicians and astrologers, but he can even tell Nebuchadnezzar, who has forgotten his dream, what he did in fact dream. Or perhaps even better, Daniel invents a dream for him, which turns out to be true. Also, Daniel is the only dream interpreter in the Bible (so far as I can see) who needs the help of someone else to interpret a dream of his own (Chapter 7). Interpreter, interpret thyself!

nation building.

There are also dream-like situations in the Bible, as when God appears in a vision, or even when we're simply told that God speaks to a character. Even this conversation (or directive) feels vision-like. Visions apparently aren't dreams, yet they often feel dream-like, or the two may meld. In Genesis 15:1-18 vision evolves into dream, when God instructs Abraham to make a sacrifice and Abraham falls asleep, and a covenant-making moment has been reached, in which dream-vision and conversation are all part of the scene. Or there are extraordinary scenes which occur in broad daylight, as when Balaam's ass "saw the angel standing in the road," an angel that finally speaks to Balaam. My friend Teresa Iverson tells me such scenes are called "waking" or "lucid dreaming."

It is sometimes hard to tell with the prophets what is vision and what is dream: "your old men shall dream dreams, your young men shall see visions" (Joel 2:28). Are dreams of lesser intensity than visions? Most famously, in what feels like a dream-vision, Isaiah is frightened and then called to his task when a seraph carries a hot coal in tongs and touches his lips with the coal, and Isaiah is thereby prepared to be a prophet (a classic example, by the way, of how the searing of the ego-lips makes the poet who he is).

The dream-vision is meant to drive the dreamer to his true life, as conveyed in Job 33:14-16, when Elihu says that through dream-visions God "openeth the ears of men, and sealeth their instruction." In the biblical dream and vision, hearing is even more important than seeing. The aural presence is a commanding sensation in the Bible.

As much as they may intrigue us, biblical dreams are a realm lost to us, or better yet, a realm that has shifted to personal discernment (that is, *psycho*-analysis). The return of what haunts us, the dream, is no longer the voice and scene that commandeers a life, as distinct from yielding insights about a life.

Furthermore, for us, the terror-stuff of dream remains private, best exemplified by its absence when we sense the prophetic moment entering our public life. Martin Luther King's "I Have a Dream Speech" re-employs the imagery of biblical visions and for us has a prophetic cast—the old imagery once more made social. He is our version of the old role; the best that we could make of it. But that concentrated visitation (in dream or vision) that is both terrifying and life-giving is not present in King's speech. That visitation of the divine-daemonic that changes a life, that terrifying dream moment that is turned into the dreamer's public role, is gone. (Though we might remember King's last address—in support of striking sanitation workers in Memphis—in which, Moses- and Jesus-like, he transcendentally foretells his impending death.) Or if it manages to return in someone who claims it, he scares us to death. The terrifying-inspiring visit from God which changes the life of the dreamer and turns him into a communal figure is what we've lost (or appears mostly in the lives of cranks, charlatans, or nuts) and that is part of what we mean when we say the age of prophecy is gone. But it was the dread of visitation—the dream or dream-like terror—that played its role *in the forming* of Abraham, Moses, and the prophets. (Maybe it's just that visions tend to come at the beginning or in the early stages of a religion, or when it's in crisis.)

So, enter art—where the terrifying visitations (the daemonic) can be converted to a shaped connection to others, turned into public discourse, a substitution, *of sorts,* for the communal implications of the individual terror-vision of the Bible. And this is part of what we mean when we invoke the Romantic idea that art replaces religion, which is both true and not true.

2003

In God's Image

Once upon a time, and several lifetimes ago, I spent the better part of a year in India, and I went to temple (in this case, temples). I was in India (at the expense of two governments) supposedly to teach American literature. But as it turns out, I really went there—like a character in a Henry James tale who visits Europe—to learn something about myself in a foreign country. Teacher, teach thyself.

Once, on visiting a temple, I saw on the floor of what seemed to be the inner sanctum, many a lingam. Shiva is often worshipped in the form of this symbolic phallus. And I suddenly found the Jew in me taken aback, not at phallic worship *per se* (I don't think), but at the idea of representing God, or gods, in the form of an image—obviously not a new idea to me, and not an idea I had not entertained from time to time (and could even half-convince myself I missed in Judaism). Yet here, suddenly, I was taken aback. So many of these stones rising from the floor, and I could not turn them into aesthetic appreciation, and thereby distance myself from their religious intent. I was surprised (and somehow, on reflection, not surprised) at my response.

I have long been intrigued by Greek mythology, never disturbed (as far as I can recall) by the power plays, rivalries and even fickleness of the Greek gods, although I could see how all this play of the gods could lead to moral dilemmas. And statues of Greek gods, or representations of the gods on vases, have always captivated me. But Greek mythology is not insisting on religious consent, whereas Hinduism, Christianity, or other living religions which can be represented by images, do make a physical-religious claim, which, however, I can usually convert to aesthetic study.

Judaism does not have a multitude of gods. (And, by the way, I have heard it argued that Hinduism is also monotheistic, with various gods or images leading the believer to the One.) Clearly, our Jewish God is not challenged by a consort, or undermined by his brothers or his children. Nor has He farmed out aspects of Himself to other gods. Of course, He *is* shown in many moods: arguing; angry; capable of changing His mind; forgiving; capable of moving from anger to pity; feeling sexual jealousy (though not engaged in sexual activity); sometimes inattentive or hard of hearing—to name a few of his characteristics. But if you wanted to put an image of the Jewish God on your dashboard, what would you put there?

Our God is monotheistic, essentially abstract, though many Jews still pray to God, who elicits their deepest desires. (To the Jewish women of Eastern Europe who uttered non-canonical Yiddish prayers, called *tkhines*, to God, He must have had a golden ear. An old saying has it that God speaks in Hebrew but listens in Yiddish, or so the speakers of Yiddish prayers would have it—a *one God* of different oral and aural powers.)

The idea of God separating into other gods and all having a physical presence does have a secret appeal to me, but only theoretically it seems. For I must confess that when actually confronted with a religious display of a multitude of gods, or the physical representation of God, the monotheistic, abstract grip of the Jewish God takes hold of me. The abstract Jewish God is almost a graven image in me, if such is possible.

I can welcome representation of God or the gods so long as I can convert those figures (i.e., figures of somebody else's religion) into contemplation. But when I'm confronted with a divine figure in a shrine or a church or some other place of worship that presses the divine presence as an immediate religious force, insisting on belief, preventing aesthetic or studious distance, I withdraw. Roadway images of Mary clad in azure and set in a white plaster niche, like a doll in a standup cradle—road-shoulder shrines that mark the places of fatal accidents—are for me intriguing and unseemly, simultaneously gross, affecting and kitschy. (I think it was Sinclair Lewis, of all people, who observed that one of the strangest things in the world is somebody else's religion.) Alas—for I do suspect there is something "alas" about the Jewish God who hunkers inside of me—my God must remain abstract, unportrayable and, of course, debatable.

And yet at times I receive images of Him that hold me: of the skirt of His robe filling the temple (Isaiah 6:1); of His hand that literally feeds Jeremiah with words (Jeremiah 1:9). Sometimes I ask myself: "What physical characteristic comes to mind when you think of God?" I don't think of His olfactory nerves (taking ritual pleasure) or of His right arm (quite strong). The only answer I have to my question is, "I think of a voice." One of the greatest religious images I know of is that of the seraph (representing God) who touches Isaiah's lips with a glowing coal gripped by tongs. And a voice of mission moves from God to Isaiah. It can make images, though it itself is not an image.

2004

The Hand of God

In offering his daughter to the mob, Lot shows himself to be a reprehensible father, and though he is saved, the Bible is quite clear about the faults of his character. Indeed, as Robert Alter deduces: "The concluding episode of this chapter, in which the drunken Lot unwittingly takes the virginity of both his daughters, suggests measure-for-measure justice meted out after his rank offer."

The scene in which Lot is saved from the mob is so physically emphatic that it might have been turned into a painting, though to the best of my knowledge it hasn't. In Alter's vivid translation:

> They had not yet lain down when the men of the city,
> the men of Sodom, surrounded the house, from lads to
> elders, every last man of them. And they called out to
> Lot and said, "Where are the men who came to you
> tonight? Bring them out to us that we may know them!"
> And Lot went out to them at the entrance, closing the
> door behind him, and he said, "Please, my brothers, do
> no harm. Look, I have two daughters who have known
> no man. Let me bring them out to you and do to them
> whatever you want. Only to these men do nothing, for
> have they not come under the shadow of my roof-beam?"
> And they said, "Step aside." And they said, "This person
> came as a sojourner and he sets himself up to judge!
> Now we'll do more harm to you than to them," and they
> pressed hard against the man Lot and moved forward
> to break down the door. And the men reached out their
> hands and drew Lot into the house and closed the door.
> And the men at the entrance of the house they struck
> with blinding light, from the smallest to the biggest,
> and they could not find the entrance.
> (Genesis 19:4-11)

The scene of the men (angels or messengers) pulling Lot back into the house, and closing the door, and then blinding the men outside the house so they couldn't find the door, grips me every time I read the passage. Their swift force takes over. What a painting that would make.

The hands of those men, messengers of God, save Lot from the hands of the men who will do him harm. That power of rescue surmounts, for the moment, the question of Lot's character (perhaps in part because there are other members of his family that could also be saved). But most of all, I imagine the hands of those angels in that scene. Those midwife-hands that save Lot in the face of disaster are what grip me, beyond any moral matter. I see those hands. I see the force of those hands, the work they have to do. That is why I am attached to this passage—the drama of the opening of the door, the reaching out, the pulling back in, the shutting out, the saving.

Those hands that reach, pull and shut remind me again of the hands of Abraham that offer bread and "a skin of water" to Hagar and then set Ishmael on her shoulders (Genesis 21:12); and the hands of Abraham that carry "the fire and the cleaver" and load the wood on the back of Isaac, and later bind him. Those hands of the angels of Sodom resonate for me, and take me to the power and puzzle of God.

Lot's offering up his daughters in the name of the greater value (the protection of his guests) reminds us of Abraham's willingness to sacrifice his son, again in the name of a calling greater than affection for one's own child. As Alter points out, both of Abraham's sons must face near-death before they can be patriarchs of a great people.

There are times when the Bible suspends moral judgment and gives us in place of such judgment the sheer force of the divine (that can take us to a deeper place than our too quick need for morality or purpose can). Sheer force is what I sense in the hands of the angels reaching for Lot and closing the door. What is that force that in this case saves but that also moves past or at least suspends moral judgment? This question of God being beyond moral categories is of course at the heart of The Book of Job. And the innocent who suffer at the hands of God's divine plan abound in the Bible. Although we have evidence God wants goodness, He can't always be counted on to follow His own advice.

The Bible often captures us because it taps into or releases energies that go beyond moral concerns. There's a powerful attraction about biblical energies that defy our own morality, and even God's, when we think we can see it. The hands of the angels at the door hold that energy for me.

Lot is saved though he doesn't deserve it, but in his survival pays for the offering up of his daughters to the mob. Abraham, on the other hand, pays no price for being responsible for the near-death of his two sons. God keeps His own moral accounts. God plays favorites. Just ask Saul.

How comforting and empowering and intoxicating it must be to forego our tense wonderment, and to reduce the vivid perplexities surrounding God to the assurances of knowing what His purposes are. Such divine confidence binds the hands of God.

2005

The Bafflement

One afternoon, I was reading the Bible on the subway, on my way to the dentist. A man next to me leaned over, smiled and said, "Ah, the Bible. You're a believer too." A mischief swept over me, and I said, "No, I'm not."

"You *don't* believe in God?" he asked, as puzzlement spread over his face.

"Nope."

"Then why do you read the Bible?"

"Because I like the stories. I love to read them. I've been reading them ever since childhood. Great stories."

He was dumbfounded, as if I had hit him over the head with the book—the Hebrew Bible, the Christian Bible, the Apocrypha, the notes and introductions, the mini-atlas, the index of names, places and themes—all in this one volume I was holding in my hands.

I went back to reading. (I don't like to be interrupted.) And just before I got up for my stop, I said to him, "Great book." He still looked disturbed and puzzled, if not a touch angry. As I went up the long, narrow escalator to the street, I was taken, and taken aback, by my *schadenfreude.*

I enjoyed my fellow-passenger's discomfort a bit too much, was indulging myself, although I knew why, tired as I was of the "true believers" who simplify these stories. My response to that man turned out to be mere position taking.

But this stranger proved to be a goad to me as much as I had been to him: "What *is* the nature of your attachment to this book?" I asked myself once again. It's like reading fiction, but it's also not like reading fiction—this book of my tribe. Its characters are and are not part of my family—like relatives I never really had. And so I go round and round about this book which, even if everything else Jewish were lost, would tell me I'm a Jew. The stories claim me. The Bible and childhood ethnicities burgeoning into quizzical indulgences and intellectual inclinations form the basis of my Jewish self. The biblical tales (especially from Genesis) seeped into me by the time I was ten or eleven, then went further through my middle age of reading, and then even further into me when I discovered the tales in the Yiddish translation by Yehoash, the poet. Possession always ran deeper than comprehension.

It is because I cannot rationalize the story of the near sacrifice of Isaac, one of the great dramatizations of God's presence, that the story has such a hold on me. I find the story grips because it has no moral justification. To be held by a story while you don't concur with what the story insists on is to face again how contradictions can be crucial to one's being, even to one's pleasure and development. And not only contradiction, but you may even be lured by a story's morality you reject—that's when things really get interesting, like my fascination with those hands saving Lot.

I have never found any interpretation of "the ordeal of Isaac" (the phrase is E. A. Speiser's) that explains its hold on me, though Kierkegaard's comparative study of faith sometimes teases me into thinking I do understand that grip, and then the prolixity of his prose clouds over the insight. Kafka comes the closest, with his parable of Abraham as the willing but unworthy believer and perpetrator—"who could not believe he was the one meant"—this vagary resonant with the distorted longing that makes Kafka the comic and religious writer he is. (Really, what do we need Woody Allen for when we have had Kafka all along?) There is something frightening about God that we hedge in with ritual, prayer, ethics, study, art, camaraderie, but that sometimes breaks through (even with the help of these "hedges"), as in the story of the near sacrifice of Isaac, at which point God's will is beyond our clarities and desires, our human connections. (A problem with much religious belief, as often noted, is that it tames God into coherence.)

To explain the story of the near sacrifice of Isaac without explaining it away, without merely using it as a confirmation of a moral attitude I possess prior to the story—that is my goal in engaging the story. I don't think I will ever achieve that goal. I don't want to relinquish the story to any moral position, including the positions that help define my life. The story has the dream-drama of the unacceptable, divinely sanctioned. This even comes across in its style, in verses 9-10, with what Speiser calls its "somnambulistic effect":

> Abraham built an altar there. He laid out the wood. He
> tied up his son Isaac. He laid him on the altar on top of
> the wood. He put out his hand and picked up the cleaver
> to slay his son.

This test of Abraham—not to align the story with our morality, but to discover the appeal of the story outside of our morality—this is what gnaws at me. I cannot solve the story—long live the story. Its power—and it is surely one of the central incidents in the entire Bible—is that it speaks to us although we cannot accept what it is saying; *that's* our attachment to it. It is about what we cannot possess and yet speaks more deeply to us than any interpretation, perhaps because it dramatizes contradiction, and we go on living with contradiction. Ah—it is diction contra diction that tries to explain the story in morally justifiable terms. What we possess is the story, not the moral. This is not a position, I think, we Jews are comfortable with.

If there is a tradition in Judaism of separating order from chaos, as has been drilled into us over and over, there is also a tradition that God created both darkness and light, the void and also life. How do you touch chaos and thereby arrive deeper into life? A squeamish sort myself, and not especially bold, I am wary of my question yet take delight in asking such a question, which implies no marching orders. The story of the near sacrifice of Isaac holds on to both terror and life. For God Himself made "water and waste and darkness" (Robert Alter's Genesis phrasing) before he went on to make all that life.

The task, I think, is not to explain the story of the near sacrifice of Isaac so that we are comfortable with it (though, contradictorily, I am a cohort of all those bound to the altar of interpretation) but to get closer to the power of the story. You can read in the newspapers about Moriah-induced nutcases, but it also strikes me that John Brown with his "streaming beard" (the phrase is Melville's) could play Abraham. Maybe he was. He looks Abrahamic. He looks like he comes out of Doré—an engraved emblem of righteousness.

With God's help (oh, fellow passenger in the subway car, I do not believe but rely on the gestures and language of belief), we make stories, make or find patterns, shape impressions—the power and surprising wealth of our perplexities—the bind that ties. And that knife Abraham holds over his son—it must be *that* knife he uses to cut the ropes that tie Isaac to the altar. What tension is dramatized here through demanding faith, following faith. God and Abraham have cut their way through their absolutes—faith confirmed and scarred, demonstrated and shocking. The strains of faith will not go away.

2006

The Bind

The near sacrifice of Isaac haunts me more than any other scene in the Bible. Unless it's Job's collapse from integrity to shock and awe; or Isaiah's lips touched by a burning coal so he can speak; or Jonah's urge to die because his ideology of God is not God; or Saul's throwing the spear at David because he, Saul (the greatest Shakespearian character in the Bible) is chosen but miserable, exalted but unworthy. I can see him visiting the "woman that hath a familiar spirit at Endor," and who channels Samuel. In childhood (entranced by Doré's engravings in my book of biblical stories, their lure of light and dark), I felt these Bible stories speaking to me—their characters a different set of relatives than the ones I knew—though I wasn't exactly sure what the stories were saying. That experience was, as it turned out, a kind of parallel to the baffling and residential presence of Yiddish. I was gifted early on with reception, from both of these sources, of what I couldn't understand. The Isaac story still plays that role.

When my grandson and I went over the story of the binding of Isaac (the subject of his bar mitzvah speech a year ago), he said that Abraham was right to follow God's command that he sacrifice his son, but that we should not be obedient in that way. When I pressed him on that split, he shrugged his way to the conclusion that what was right in the Bible is not necessarily right for us. I could do no better than leave him with his contradictions, as I am left with mine, as God is with His, calling on Abraham to sacrifice his son but Himself pulling back at the last minute.

Fate, character, and training make me for and not against interpretation (even though I also yearn for that "against"), yet I cannot reach an interpretation which does justice to this story and to my imagination. The story defeats me precisely as it captures me. Explanations of the story in historical terms (while usually enlightening, and sometimes even possessing an aura of their own) do not finally satisfy me, or account for the hold the story has on me—the personal grip. As much as I profit from exegesis I myself am an addict of eisegesis, a word waiting for me to find it, as I did recently.* In my way I am a fundamentalist reader of the Bible.

When I say I am defeated by a story (like this one) I mean that I do not understand why it grips me. To be defeated by a story is not the same as saying, "Well, I don't understand this, and I don't want to bother trying to. I give up on it." To be defeated by a story (or a poem or a painting) is to succumb to what you cannot comprehend, or to be in a state where comprehension is an inkling. The story stays in you *because* it is not fully grasped. And it can reside inside of you your entire life in that condition. It won't release you, nor fully reveal itself to you. It has reached a stage more compelling than understanding or comprehension. Maybe that's what Yeats meant when he wrote in a letter shortly before he died, "Man can embody truth but he cannot know it."

And then one morning, just before I got out of bed, it dawned on me (one of the blessings of sleep) that the story of the near sacrifice of Isaac dramatizes a religious tension: God put aside His own command for ritual killing and commanded the preservation of life. God exists in contradiction. It is as if God said to us: "Enter Me in My contradictions. This is the life I have given you." It is often said that we don't know what God wants. Yet sometimes He is quite clear about what He wants, and some of the time wants the opposite of what He wants before, or at least something different. But maybe that's another way of saying that we don't know what He wants. I think, finally, that we want something more than understanding. Job never reaches understanding, never, of course, gets justice, never comprehends what has happened to him. But he is engaged

---

* *Eisegesis* – "an interpretation, especially of Scripture, that expresses the interpreter's own ideas, bias, or the like, rather than the meaning of the text." In other words, as the prefixes apprise—a reading into, *eis*egesis, rather than a reading out of, *ex*egesis. On discovering the word I felt less like the Adam who had named the animals than an Adam who had identified some creature within himself.

in uttering his case. And God prefers him to all those explainer away'ers—the pious knowers. And why shouldn't He, for Job is closer to God.

Reading Louis Ginzberg's *The Legends of the Jews* (a *Gesta Judaica*) has taken me deeper into the tale of Abraham and Isaac. The function of the legends in this instance, I suspect, is to ease the terror of the story.

We are told that every part of the carcass of the sacrificed ram was put to some use, including, "Of the sinews of the ram, David made ten strings for his harp upon which he played." And here we have the makings of a Jewish equivalent of the Orpheus legend. (A bone of Orpheus is turned into a flute). Out of this terrifying story comes David playing music.

I don't thereby conclude with an indulgent aesthetic leap out of a moral dilemma produced by the story of the binding of Isaac. On the contrary, the physical source of David's music making only increases our awareness of contradiction, of our dilemma—the tension between the making of beauty and our sense of terror. The music of David is literally tuned by the substitute sacrifice.

In one of the legends shaped by Ginzberg, God Himself grows from this event, learning a thing or two. Abraham compels God to forgive Israel for its trespasses in the future. (The return of the combative Abraham.) God accedes, saying that He will do so when He hears that ram's horn (another use of the slaughtered ram) the day of the New Year, appreciating that the ram was sacrificed in place of Isaac. Abraham extracts this promise from God because of the suffering he and Isaac went through on Mount Moriah. It is as if Abraham shames God into forgiveness, and those later inventors, the makers of the legends, have eased the terror of the story, and expanded on the character of God.

Given the terror and the complexities and the dilemmas inherent in this story (and in many others in the Bible), I imagine I can understand, even appreciate (though I risk condescension at this moment) the ease and the need with which some people glide from biblical tale to moral certitude. In the legend, God acknowledges Abraham's right to press Him into forgiveness, as if God wants to get Himself off the hook. What *is* our religion once we acknowledge that the force of those biblical tales lies in the composition of our dilemmas? God Himself is affected by the human condition He has created. God browbeats Job, but He is also the potter who is as much subject to the wheel of change as the clay itself. He is also the force who refuses to reveal the truth to Job.

The story of the near sacrifice of Isaac, however, finally defeats me (though I may win a skirmish, or think I do, here and there). Some (most? all?) of the stories that captivate us do so precisely because they leap beyond our moral view. They are superior to our values, to our constructions, and *thereby* speak to us, taking us to even deeper places, and we can be both possessed and dislocated by such works.

I am not satisfied with any of the explanations of the story of the binding of Isaac. But I am compelled to read it again and again. I don't understand why this story grips me so. I am taken by a drama whose moral basis I cannot accept. But—and this is the "inkling" I dropped in earlier—the story grips me, I think, because I am fascinated by a faith that I cannot bring myself to, and this story, perhaps more than any other biblical tale, tells me what I lack religiously, what I shall never have; and therefore God and prayer and ritual will always be for me the participation in a longing that must finally be aborted because my religion is really—void and grappling. And for that there is also a biblical tale. Yet even this stance risks a kind of moral self-congratulation, an aloof pride posing as intellectual courage. For the tale's greatest allure, paradox, and danger is the notion that the follower of God who is willing to lose all (embodied by Isaac) is the one who is blessed. My attraction to the story startles itself.

2008

Return to Yiddish

The recognition scene in Chapter 45 of Genesis plays itself out in the conversation between Joseph and his brothers, that is, in the language from the land they all come from—a language which is not Egyptian, but a language from the old country, and this is the language we will hear as I switch from the King James Version to Yehoash's Yiddish version. (I choose these two translations because they are for me irreplaceable, the two translations that my ears love.) I imagine Joseph and his brothers and his father speaking Yiddish among themselves as they are being brought into the larger Egyptian sphere of speech and political power. I have added fiction to fiction as I possess the story, fabricating a transgressive translation of my own, approximating the story's duality of language.

Joseph clears the receiving room of everyone but himself and his brothers and cries—and how he cries, in his rich garments, with not a single Egyptian present, a scene worthy of Rembrandt. The Egyptians behind the doors hear his weeping and some strange language muffled by those doors.

"I am Joseph, doth my father yet live?"

"Ikh bin yoysef, lebt nokh mayn foter?"

(It's a pity that Yehoash didn't use the more redolent *tatn*, rather than *foter*. Or perhaps this is a trace of some distance still existing between Joseph and his family, also suggested in the rhetorical nature of the question, for he already knows that Jacob lives. The question has the air of a gambit about it—Joseph being Joseph.)

How astonished the brothers are at that assertion of a blood tie, stunned not only by the claim but *by the sound of it*—not in Egyptian but in their common language, Yiddish. The language of delivery—not a target language, but a language with a target, them, the brothers—here penetrates even more deeply than the content, sound itself its own proof. The filial claim is something, but the language is a stunner, even as it tries to mollify their amazement and fear by inviting them to come closer:

> "Come near to me, I pray you."

> *"Genent tsu mir, ikh bet aykh."*

And they come (and we must imagine, trembling) as Joseph repeats and adds, as reinforcement (which must make them tremble even more), only what they would know,

> "I am Joseph your brother, whom ye sold into Egypt."

> *"Ikh bin ayer bruder yoysef, vos ihr hot mikh farkoyft keyn mitzrayim."*

He adds now "your brother"/ *"ayer bruder"* (a touch formal that *"ayer"*), and the place name, his narrative also superior to what they could have known.

Joseph sees they're frightened (probably knowing they would be) and tries to reassure them that he does not reveal himself in order to do them harm,

> "Now, therefore, be not grieved, nor angry with yourselves, that you have sold me hither: for God did send me before you to preserve life."

> *"Un atsind zolt ihr aykh nit klemen, un zol nit fardrisn in ayere oygn, vos ihr hot mikh farkoyft aher, vorum tsu derhaltn lebm hot mikh got farshikt aykh faroys."*

The theological rationalization is absorbed into the brewing of family feelings. The writer of this story is a master of synchronicity.

Hearing such pleading Yiddish from a man who goes on to

claim himself "a father to pharaoh and lord of all his house, and a ruler throughout all the land of Egypt"—how could the brothers believe their ears? Except that they might have detected a touch of the old (I mean young) boastful Joseph.

Joseph reassures and reassures that he is no mirage:

"And, behold, your eyes see, and the eyes of my brother Benjamin, that it is my mouth that speaketh unto you."

"Un ot zeyen ayere oygn, un di oygn fun mayn bruder benyomin, az mayn moyl redt dokh tsu aykh."

How then can they deny this tribal language coming from the mouth of this man their brother, no matter how he's dressed amid the rich surroundings? (And part of their punishment is that they have to stomach the singling out of Benjamin, in Joseph's handling of the narration.)

And then the weeping and weeping on all sides—again the singling out of Joseph's tie to Benjamin, the necks of Joseph and Benjamin wet with tears, only afterwards Joseph kissing the others.

"And after that his brethren talked with him."

"Un dernokh hot zayne brider geredt mit ihm."

The gabble and tie of the old family speech insinuate themselves among them.

They talked "with a father to pharaoh" in Yiddish, and Yiddish was heard by the servants and bureaucrats though they weren't sure what they were hearing—some kind of language. And Joseph, now speaking and hearing the language after so many years, perhaps even associating his misery with it, must have been as shaken by its sounds as were his brothers.

The emotive Joseph, however, has never been entirely divorced from the shrewd Joseph (a similar strain existing in his father). For after bestowing provisions, clothes, wagons, money (to Benjamin), gifts for his father, he makes his last remark, shrewdly and even guilt-inducing, "See that you fall not by the way."

"Ihr zolt aykh nit krign afn veg."

Joseph's Yiddish never felt heavier upon their ears.

And they return to their father and tell him what had happened, and what was said, *in Yiddish, in Egypt.* (I wish I were a fly on the wall to hear them broach and then narrate the whole thing.) Jacob couldn't believe his ears, nearly fainting. But finally he takes it all in:

> "And Israel said, It is enough; my son Joseph is yet alive: I
> will go and see him before I die."

> "Un yisroyel hot gezogt: Genug! Mayn zun yoysef lebt nokh; ihk
> vel geyen un veln ihm zen eyder ikh shtarb . . ."

Jacob's *"mayn zun yoysef lebt nokh"* echoing Joseph's *"lebt nokh mayn foter?"*

The emotion of the recognition scene (or scenes) cannot be separated from the switch by Joseph and his brothers to Yiddish, their mother tongue, or, their mothers' tongue. The language in which Joseph spoke was as important as what he said, strains absorbed by the shocked, fearful, and then convinced brothers. The recognitions penetrate into the very sounds of speech—speech, the marker of their fright, their amazement, reconciliation, as if their very weeping were done in Yiddish. In returning to the language of his youth—redolent with arrogance and betrayal and danger—Joseph also finds a new voice, which is a new self in that old voice, the mother tongue, and confirms a tie to those he had looked down upon in his youth.

2010